Effortless Beauty

PHOTOGRAPHY AS AN EXPRESSION OF
EYE, MIND AND HEART

Effortless Beauty

PHOTOGRAPHY AS AN EXPRESSION OF
EYE, MIND AND HEART

Julie DuBose

Miksang
PUBLICATIONS

Miksang Publications
Boulder, Colorado

www.miksangpublications.com

© 2013 by Julie DuBose

All rights reserved. No part of this book may be reproduced in any form or by any means, electronic or mechanical, including photocopying, recording, or by any information storage and retrieval system, without permission in writing from the publisher.

9 8 7 6 5 4 3 2 1

First Edition

Printed in China

Designed by Dayna Schueth

ISBN 978-0-9859774-0-5

Follow your pure heart
Let your eye and mind float together as one
In the experience of resting in openness and simplicity
The visual world manifests as Effortless Beauty.

Julie DuBose

Contents

Introduction

1. The Birthplace of Unconditional Expression — 1
2. Learning to See Through Letting Go — 9
3. Hot, Joyful, and Ripe: Perception Beyond Thought — 17
   Openness, Genuineness, Confidence
4. True Perception, True Expression — 27
5. Cultivating a Mind of Simplicity — 35
   Fully Present, Free from Self Absorption and Distraction
6. The Main Ingredients: Stillness and Intention — 43
7. Developing New Sight — 51
8. Flashes of Lightning — 57
9. Coming to a Full Stop — 65
10. Developing Trust in Our Experience — 73
11. Resting Fully in Our Perception — 81
12. The Image as Completion — 89
13. Unwound and Relaxed — 95
    The Pause that Refreshes
14. Intimate Seeing: Engaging the Body and Mind — 109
15. The Gateway to Perception: Dissolving Boredom — 115
16. Making Contact — 123
17. Exploring Fields of Perception — 133

18	Sad Joy	141
	Seeing as Receiving	
	The Smile of Recognition	
	The Tender Open Heart	
	Resonance	
19	The Heat of Direct Perception	153
	The Door is Open	
	Falling in Love	
20	Visually Conscious Living: Making Room for Beauty in Our Lives	161
	Paying Attention	
	Being Deliberate is a Lifestyle Choice	
	Ordinary World, Ordinary Magic	
	The Pond	
	Our Home is a Palace	
21	Essential Simplicity	181
	Keeping it Fresh	
	Working with the Obstacle of Continuous Distraction	
	How the Practice of Conscious Seeing Disrupts Continuous Distraction	
	Allowing Ourselves the Space to Be Undistracted	
	Keeping it Fresh/Working with Uncertainty	
22	Image Viewing as Practice	195
	Editing is a Reflection of Our State of Mind	
23	When Direct Seeing Becomes Part of Who You Are	205
24	The Fully Met Life	213

About the Author

Acknowledgements

Further Resources

Notes on the Photographs

Introduction

"There is a crack, a crack in everything. That's how the light gets in."
Leonard Cohen

If we could live our lives in freshness, discovering our world anew everyday, and share that with our loved ones, would that be worth doing? If we could look at our partners and see them completely and deeply, would we be able to love them more fully? If we could look at snow falling on the pavement and feel its gentle softness on our face, would we simply enjoy the experience without our habitual dread of cold, snowy days? Could we discover the brilliant colors in our world and simply enjoy? We could live this way. We can learn to see simply and completely, without our thoughts continually separating us from the freshness of our experience. And we can develop our ability to express these experiences through our photographs.

In the world of photography, advances in digital technology have made taking vivid, sharp photographs easy to do. We now have the possibility to express the experience of our world without having to learn a lot about the technical aspects of photography.

We can shoot on automatic mode and have all the decisions about how to take the photo made for us. Anyone who has an eye, mind, and the desire to communicate can shoot high-quality photographs.

This new opportunity brings up new questions: What do I do with this technological wonder? Shoot my friends and family? If I go on a trip, I can photograph the historic sites and points of interest to show my friends back home. I can shoot the most famous places the same way everyone who has been there before me has done. And if I am adventurous, I can create very cool images in digital editing programs such as Photoshop.

I can shoot anything I want and from that, create something totally different, a work of creative art. I can make adjustments to darken, lighten, change the color, and paste in other elements to create a totally new image. Whatever I can think of, I can create in Photoshop.

What if we took a different approach to expressing what we see through photography? Have you had moments when you see something so new, so fresh, that you can't believe it, something so outside of your box that you could never have imagined it? The world we live in is a very rich place, visually. When we take the time to really notice the details of what we are seeing, there is an infinite realm of visual experience waiting for us to explore. Rather than judging what is best or right, good or bad, about what we are seeing, why not set out to explore exactly what is in front of us, wherever we are?

There are many photography courses about the technical use of the camera, photographic rules, and templates of acceptable subject matter. But it is extremely rare to find a teacher who can show us how to photograph in an authentic and fresh new way. For our images to successfully and completely communicate our perception, we have to understand what we have seen. To really express our experience, we have to take a leap beyond all of the ideas we have about what we are seeing.

We have to open our minds and pay very close attention to our world, like visitors to another culture, with very different language, customs, and appearance. We can leave our baggage in our hotel room and wander freely through this new world. What we see has the flavor of being seen for the first time, without the labels and categorization of experience that we usually impose on whatever we see.

We do not have to travel to have this experience of newness and wonder. The richness that we have inherited as human beings is all around us, in the direct experience of the forms in our world: colors, textures, lines light. It is ours to enjoy, to appreciate, if we can be present to see it. It is in our kitchens, our bedrooms, our offices, on our walks, as we look at friends and loved ones.

This is our world. It has a heart beat and our blood runs through it, like a river of life and feeling, with qualities of hard, soft, wet, smooth, full, empty, lonely, and joyful. We can express the experience of direct living with our camera. We may not be sure what our expressions mean, but they will be real, the genuine article. The photograph will carry within it our heart, our mind, the blood of our experience.

This book is a road map of a path for taking different kinds of photographs, which might even lead to a different kind of living: direct living through direct seeing. The images are expressions of moments of direct perceptions for me. As you look at the images, you are looking through my eyes, my mind, and my heart. I am sharing with you, and so will you share with others. May it bring you deep enjoyment!

INTRODUCTION

EFFORTLESS BEAUTY

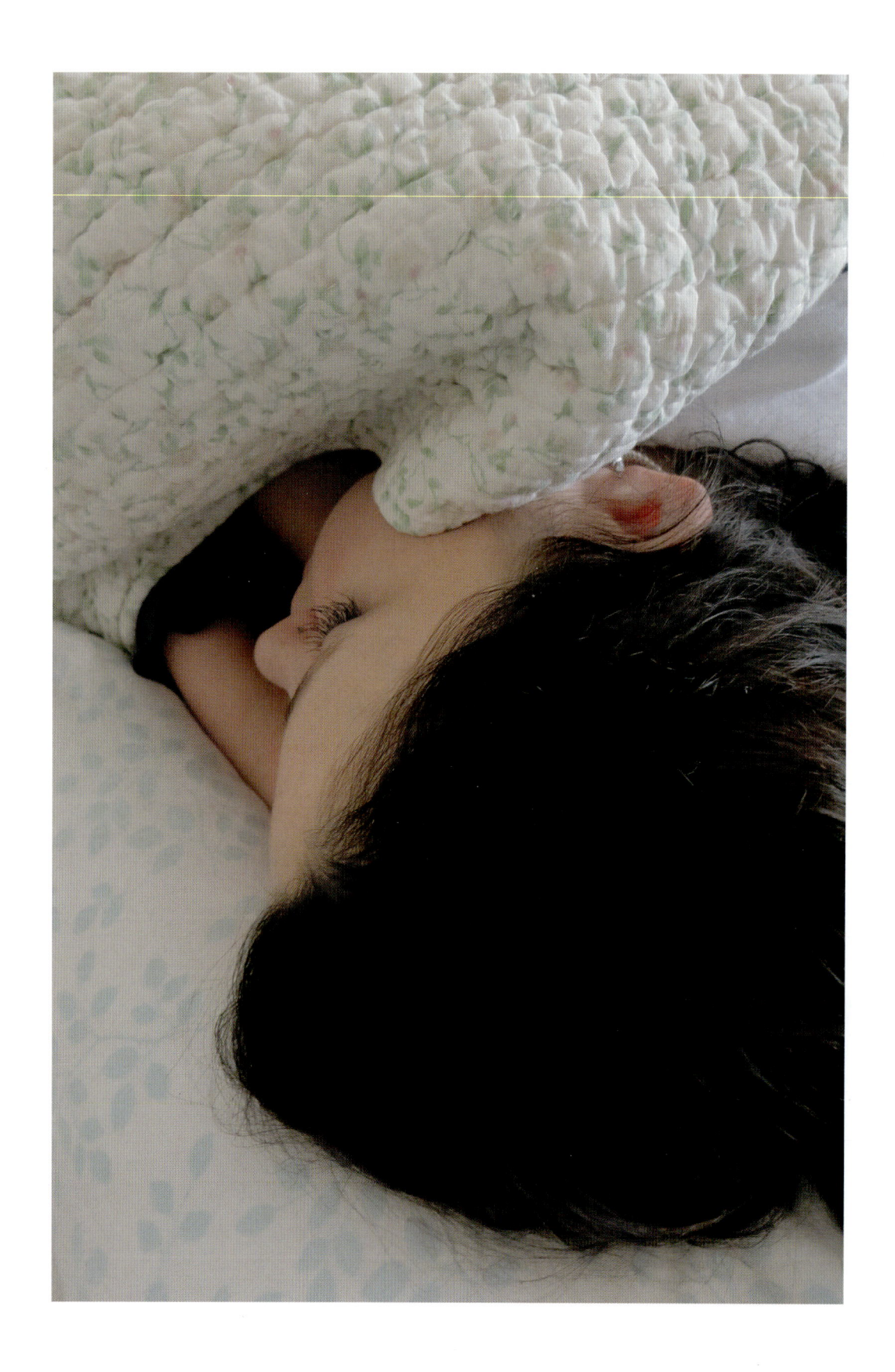

INTRODUCTION

EFFORTLESS BEAUTY

INTRODUCTION

1 THE BIRTHPLACE OF UNCONDITIONAL EXPRESSION

"There is such a thing as unconditional expression,
That does not come from self or other.
It manifests out of nowhere,
Like mushrooms in a meadow,
Like hailstorms, like thundershowers."

Chögyam Trungpa.
The Art of Calligraphy

In the experience of writing this book I've come to realize how similar the process of writing is to shooting photographs. When we want to write something, we start with a blank sheet of paper. This is our canvas. We have to start somewhere. Do we start with a lot of smart ideas about what we want to say? Or do we start from the canvas of our open state of mind with an intention to express our experience, and perhaps our wisdom? This is the dividing line where we choose to make art from our direct experience, or art from our conceptual ideas.

The impulse, the desire to communicate, is present. The potential is percolating in our minds. Then the words emerge from within us. We speak with our own voice and what we say feels like truth, like a deep rumble beneath the earth, like piercing sunlight. It is our experience.

If we begin with an open, receptive, curious, attentive mind, free of judgment and the desire to interpret, the impulse to express will flow through us, vibrating with possibility. From this openness, unconditional expression is born.

It is also the same process as writing songs. When I am ready to write a song, I have a feeling it is time to give birth. I know it. I can feel it. The vibration is happening, and I can't do anything else until I get the song out, until I make it whole, until it is here with me.

So I have to make myself available for the inspiration to come through. I have to sit down and be, maybe start playing a few chords to link up with the process. Somehow, when I know what the first step is, when I know where it begins, then I begin. What comes out first, the beginning of the expression process, may not be the beginning. It may be the middle. I have to find my way through it, but always while staying out of the way so it can unfold. It is a calibration. You are calibrating yourself so that whatever it is that you want to express is lined up with being in the present moment.

You are aligned with your heart and mind, your being, your intention, with the present moment, and with what is waiting to come forth. It's true whether we are writing a song, writing a book, telling a story, or taking a photograph. It's a three- way conference call between what is being expressed, the present moment, and our heart and mind.

In the case of direct visual perception, the state of openness in our minds is like the blank sheet of paper. Blankness is vibrating with presence, with possibility, with the willingness to connect. It is the birthplace of direct perception, where all unconditional perception and expression occurs. To prepare ourselves to see, we dissolve our thoughts into our sense of being fully present in the only moment that we have, the one that is right now. All other moments have ceased, or have not yet happened. This is all we have.

So we feel this moment, in our bodies, in our breath, in our awareness of the ground, the pavement, and in our arms, legs, and the texture of our clothing. We feel all this and we feel fully alive.

Just like that, when we are ready, when the time is right, the space is prepared, and we have our instruments of expression, the energy of creation begins to flow, sometimes with a few bumps in the way, but it starts to come out. All we have to do is get out of the way. We don't want to think too much about what's happening. We just want to be aware of it and be fully there. So whatever the factors are that are coming together—timing, placement, space, light—we don't do anything to interfere, to stop it, to move outside of it, to second-guess it, or to look at it from the outside. When we observe what is happening and make comments about it, the thoughts and comments actually become obstacles to the flow of creation.

Doing this allows for a depth of expression that is far more alive than anything we could think up. When we are photographing, if we begin with an idea of what we would like to see, such as, "I want to go out and shoot some nature today," or "I would like to find some really great red flowers," we will very likely see only that, and little else. Our experience will be limited, and not fresh.

It is much more effective in the creation of an unconditional expression if we start out with no thought whatsoever. In the case of photography, for us to have an unconditional visual expression, we first need to have an unconditional perception. So how do we do this?

The first thing that we do is to find our ground. We bring our mind into the present moment. This moment is the ground for the whole experience. Our mind is present and available. What does this mean? It means that we are not thinking about anything else but being here right now and the possibility of connecting, of communicating with whatever it is that stops our mind. That openness is the ground.

From this we prepare to go forth, to experience whatever meets us. And then it happens. Out of nowhere comes a meeting of light, color, texture, line.

We don't know what it is that we have seen. We have no idea. But that is OK. We don't need to know. In the present moment we are with our new friend. We can take our time and get acquainted. We don't have any expectation that we will know anything beyond the experience happening right now. It is magical because it came out of nowhere. It is fresh because we didn't make it up.

EFFORTLESS BEAUTY

THE BIRTHPLACE OF UNCONDITIONAL EXPRESSION

EFFORTLESS BEAUTY

THE BIRTHPLACE OF UNCONDITIONAL EXPRESSION

2 Learning to See Through Letting Go

Becoming visually conscious does not involve adding to our body of conceptual knowledge. It involves letting go of our habitual patterns, our ways of labeling and sorting everything we experience, and in this case, everything we see.

We begin our lives experiencing without association or reference points. We don't know what anything that we see means. Gradually as we develop through our lives, we build a complex mental network of connections, contexts, and relative meaning and value. We could call this network the Central Processing Unit. When we learn, we incorporate the new material into the body of knowledge we have accumulated. Whatever we see is experienced by us through this elaborate filtering system of likes and dislikes, preferences of all kinds. Using a computer analogy once more, we could say that our personal preference file pre-sorts and labels everything we see.

The classification and organization of our experience happens very quickly, so quickly in fact that rarely do we realize that we are doing it.

However, we have been visually conscious before. As infants, seeing was part of our sensory awareness. When we would see, we experienced with all of our senses at once; they were not separated into feeling, hearing, and seeing. And we experienced sensation in a full-bodied way, with our entire being. Within each of us we hold the innate ability to experience the world directly and fully once again. In our courses we do visual exercises to reestablish our connection to the experience of direct seeing, to remind us of the way we perceived things before we learned their meaning.

When our conceptual mind goes off-line for an instant, we are there, and our experience is fresh and startling. There is a short circuit in our preference file, an opening occurs, and the light shines through.

We have an innate ability to connect unconditionally with our world. This means that we can be wide open and receptive, free of ideas and preferences. We can work directly with our world with our wisdom guiding us.

This wisdom or knowing does not arise from inference or reasoning but instead from a basic sensitivity about how things fit together in relationship. We have deep, non-conceptual ways of sensing that we use to navigate between objects, to sense how things feel, to perceive the qualities of things and the qualities of our experience.

This wisdom is a fundamental part of who we are and how we understand our world and the profound messages that come from connecting with it. It often lies buried beneath our insecurities and the worldviews we have adopted from our life education.

We are going to dedicate our intention to uncover and activate this sense of natural wisdom so we can function as natural, unencumbered human beings. This is a process of letting go; letting go of what we think we know, letting go of all our conventional ideas and concepts that we have always relied upon. Letting go, letting go, letting go, so that we can experience the wisdom that is inherent in our minds, that is awake, inquisitive, and dynamically engaged in the experience of living our lives. The only way to access this wisdom is to let go. There is no other way. When we function within our innate wisdom, beyond our sense of qualification and limitation, when we free ourselves of our ideas about our experience, we become visually conscious.

"Wisdom cannot be born from theory; it must be born from your actual state of mind, which is the working basis for all spiritual practice. The wisdom of dealing with situations as they are, and that is what wisdom is, contains tremendous precision that could not come from anywhere else but the physical situations of sight, smell, feeling, touchable objects, and sounds. The earthy situation of actual things as they are is the source of wisdom. You can become completely one with smell, with sight, with sound, and your knowledge about them ceases to exist; your knowledge becomes wisdom."

Chögyam Trungpa
Glimpses of Abhidharma

LEARNING TO SEE THROUGH LETTING GO 12

13   EFFORTLESS BEAUTY

LEARNING TO SEE THROUGH LETTING GO   14

EFFORTLESS BEAUTY

LEARNING TO SEE THROUGH LETTING GO   16

3 Hot, Joyful, and Ripe: Perception Beyond Thought

What does it mean to really see? It means that we are free from forethought or afterthought. We don't think about what we want to see and then go find it. When we do have a visual perception, we don't think about how we can improve upon it by adding elements that were not part of the perception to make it more "interesting," more "attractive." When we have forethought or afterthought, we are putting conditions on our perceptions. Whether we go find something to photograph that conforms to an idea we have of what we think we would like to shoot, or whether we begin with an actual perception and then modify it afterwards, the resulting image becomes our idea of what we saw.

We have to make room in our minds for a perception to occur. We prepare ourselves so we can be fully present, fully aware of what we are seeing, so that when it happens, we will know it. If we were warriors, preparing to go into battle, knowing that our survival could depend upon being fully and properly prepared, we would put all thoughts of yesterday and tomorrow out of our minds. We would tell ourselves that there is no other moment than this one. We would rouse our intention to be watchful, awake, and fully disciplined. We would make sure that our weapons were fully functional. We would allow no thought that might distract, pull our awareness from the present moment.

And so it is with unconditional perception. We prepare ourselves by bringing our awareness to our bodies, to our minds. We let our thoughts go as we relax into the sensation of our body and the earth beneath our feet. We let our thoughts come and go without following them. As our mind becomes still and relaxed, we establish our intention to see. We turn our awareness out to the visual world.

Then, out of nowhere, a perception dawns. It is unconditional because it does not come from a thought or a strategy of what or how to see. It happens because we have prepared ourselves properly to be open, genuine, and confident.

Openness

The discipline and practice of direct seeing has three primary ingredients: Openness, Genuineness, and Confidence. An open state of mind provides the room and the possibility for a meeting on neutral ground. In fact, it is within this space of openness that perceptions arise in our minds. Without that open state of mind we cannot see anything beyond the instant overlay of our own likes and dislikes, preferences, associations, and memories. In short we can't see anything as it truly is.

When we go out on a photographic expedition, we are explorers in the best sense, setting out willing to be met fully, to understand, and to appreciate. We have to let go of our fear and uncertainty, to abandon our credentials and our preconditions. We could consider ourselves to be the best photographer we know, or maybe we are afraid that we are going to embarrass ourselves. But in the world of direct seeing we suspend the rules of safe conduct that govern our behavior. We explore the visual world with an open mind and heart.

Genuineness

We all have the ability to be touched deeply by our experiences. It is an aspect of our humanity that keeps us real and honest. Being touched happens when we aren't expecting anything and when we have surrendered the struggle with our circumstances. We have to give up the desire to be better, to be special, to be number one, or even the last one. Our genuineness comes through when we relax our protective guard, and our need to cover up or hide because we don't accept that we are good enough.

We have everything we need in our basic makeup to have splendid, brilliantly vivid perceptions. We have eyes, mind, and heart. We have the desire to connect our visual sense directly with the world. We want our experience to be the real thing, not diminished by meaningless distractions and a sense of uncertainty. We want it hot, joyful, and ripe with the fullness of being alive. When we bring all these elements together in one moment, we will indeed have profound visual experiences beyond anything we could think up or imagine. This is the basis of authentic, genuine perception.

Most of us don't need to be told what genuineness is. We have had experiences that resonated deeply within us. We can remember moments when our mind and eye were suddenly caught upon a color, a beam of light. Our thoughts ceased and nothing else existed but that beam of light in that moment.

When we are being genuine, we don't feel like we have to make up the most amazing things to photograph, and we don't have to be "the best photographer." We want to be able to photograph the world around us, the ordinary yet preciously singular moments when the sun pours across our kitchen sink and we see soft color against smooth tile, folded dishcloths stacked in the sun, radiating vivid color. We all know these simple perceptions. They express our everyday lives with the simplicity of no elaboration.

There are two aspects to genuineness in relation to photography. We are good enough to trust ourselves and to express our experience. With our eye, mind, and heart we have what we need already within us as human beings. We know we can be ourselves without embarrassment and a sense of having to measure up. We can feel this genuineness in ourselves.

The second aspect is that when we truly see the world directly, the way it presents itself to us is fully complete. It is just as it is, and we are simply as we are. The two can come together and meet in a moment of awareness. Afterwards, as we look at the image we have taken of this moment, we don't have to fix or improve upon what we have seen, make it more interesting to our friends. It's perfect simply as it is.

Confidence

It takes discipline and frequently it takes some bravado to be genuine, to avoid feeling like we are the hunter and our visual world is our prey. We have moments when we aren't involved in covering up our genuineness, in which we can be still and appreciate what we have seen. At some point though, we pull back and begin to evaluate, to judge. We are pulled by our habitually restless mind to look around and evaluate our perception by looking at it from outside our experience. Then we begin to compare and contrast, superimpose the criteria of other photographers we have reason to think are respected by others, and so on. Sometimes the perception gets lost. We actually lose it in the maze of our internal dialogue. When we realize that we no longer can see the original perception, there is a moment of confusion and futility. We have to be willing to abandon our mental restlessness and come back to the basic authentic perception.

This is our discipline, how we develop our stability of genuineness. We come back over and over again to our perception. We learn to discriminate between our value judgments and overlays on the one hand, and the simplicity of the perception that has arisen on the other. It is the thread that holds and binds the integrity, the truth, of our experience. This thread is like a lifeline in a big ocean. The waves could carry us away, but the lifeline stays still and does not waver. We can maintain our connection to the perception.

As we work with the discipline of coming back to it again and again, we develop trust and confidence in ourselves. We begin to know without question that we can recognize when our eye and mind have been stopped by a moment of genuine perception. We know how that feels and what happens in our minds and what the flavor of it is. We have confidence in our unshakeableness because we don't need to prove anything.

21 EFFORTLESS BEAUTY

HOT, JOYFUL, AND RIPE: PERCEPTION BEYOND THOUGHT   22

23 EFFORTLESS BEAUTY

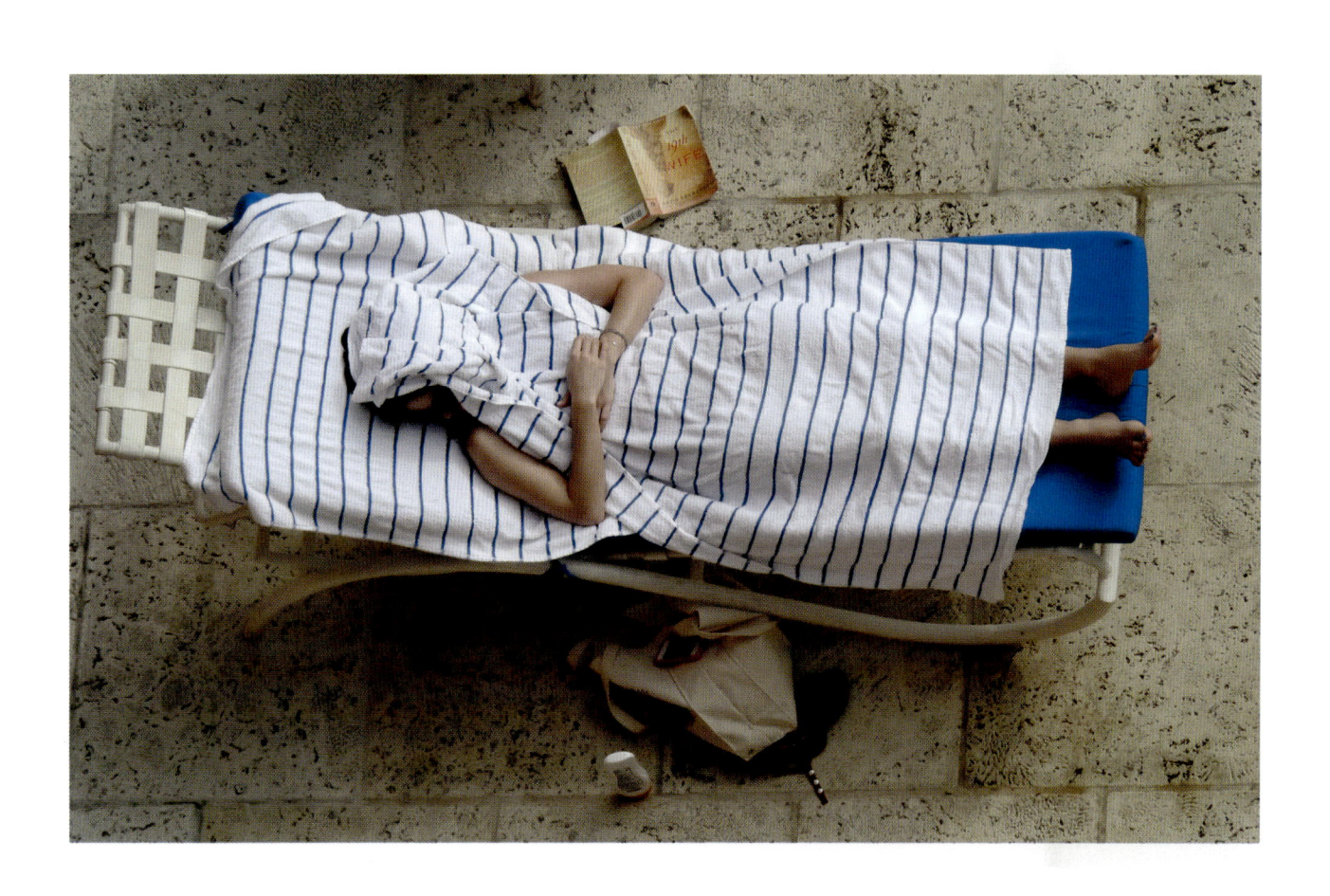

HOT, JOYFUL, AND RIPE: PERCEPTION BEYOND THOUGHT   24

25 EFFORTLESS BEAUTY

HOT, JOYFUL, AND RIPE: PERCEPTION BEYOND THOUGHT   26

4   True Perception, True Expression

There are many reasons that someone becomes motivated to develop their ability to have vivid, fresh perceptions and express them in their photographs. Perhaps they have experienced direct visual perceptions and have been moved by the uniqueness and vividness of the perception. They would like to be able to develop the ability to see this way all the time.

Also along these lines, someone has had direct perceptions, but find they are unable to translate those into their photographs. The final image is missing the quality and the directness of the original perception.

Sometimes there is a strong desire to connect with the visual world and express what is seen. But it can be difficult, if we don't have fresh perceptions of our own, to figure out what to shoot. Many of us seek safe ground by imitating photographs someone else has taken that we have seen at a gallery or in a book.

There is a sense of vagueness about what we could really see for ourselves if we looked. Would it be boring, would it be good enough that people would like it?

Seasoned photographers can grow tired of their database of familiar perceptions and images. They want to see outside of their box.

They find the expensive equipment, complicated rules, and endlessly evolving technology become a burden, no longer a medium for joyful expression. They are missing the freshness of discovery, the passion of connection. Sometimes it takes getting sick of one's habitual ways of seeing and expressing to open up to new approaches.

Regardless of how much previous photographic experience we have, we have to be prepared to open our minds, start at the beginning, and lay the ground properly, so that nothing gets lost and the essential ingredients for direct seeing are fully present and activated. To see directly, all we need is our mind, our eye, and our intention to see.

Because we have invested our lifetime in developing our worldview, the willingness to change can be tentative in the beginning. There is a saying, "If we do what we have always done, we'll get what we've always gotten." If we are willing to put into practice what we learn from this approach, we will have brilliant, vivid perceptions and express them completely.

For all of us, regardless of how far we go down this road, the journey we take will leave a lasting impact upon how we see and experience our world for as long as we live.

29 EFFORTLESS BEAUTY

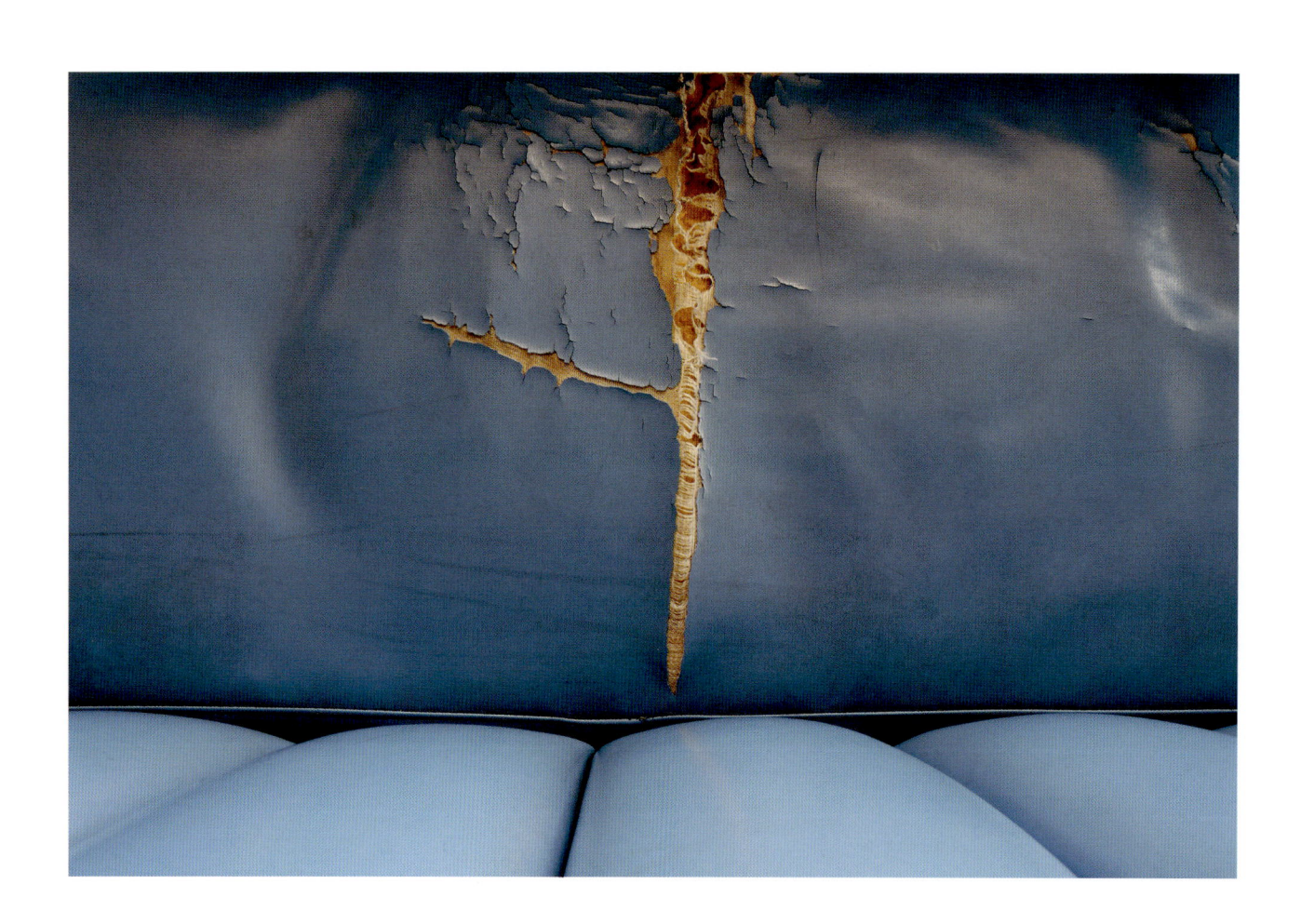

TRUE PERCEPTION, TRUE EXPRESSION

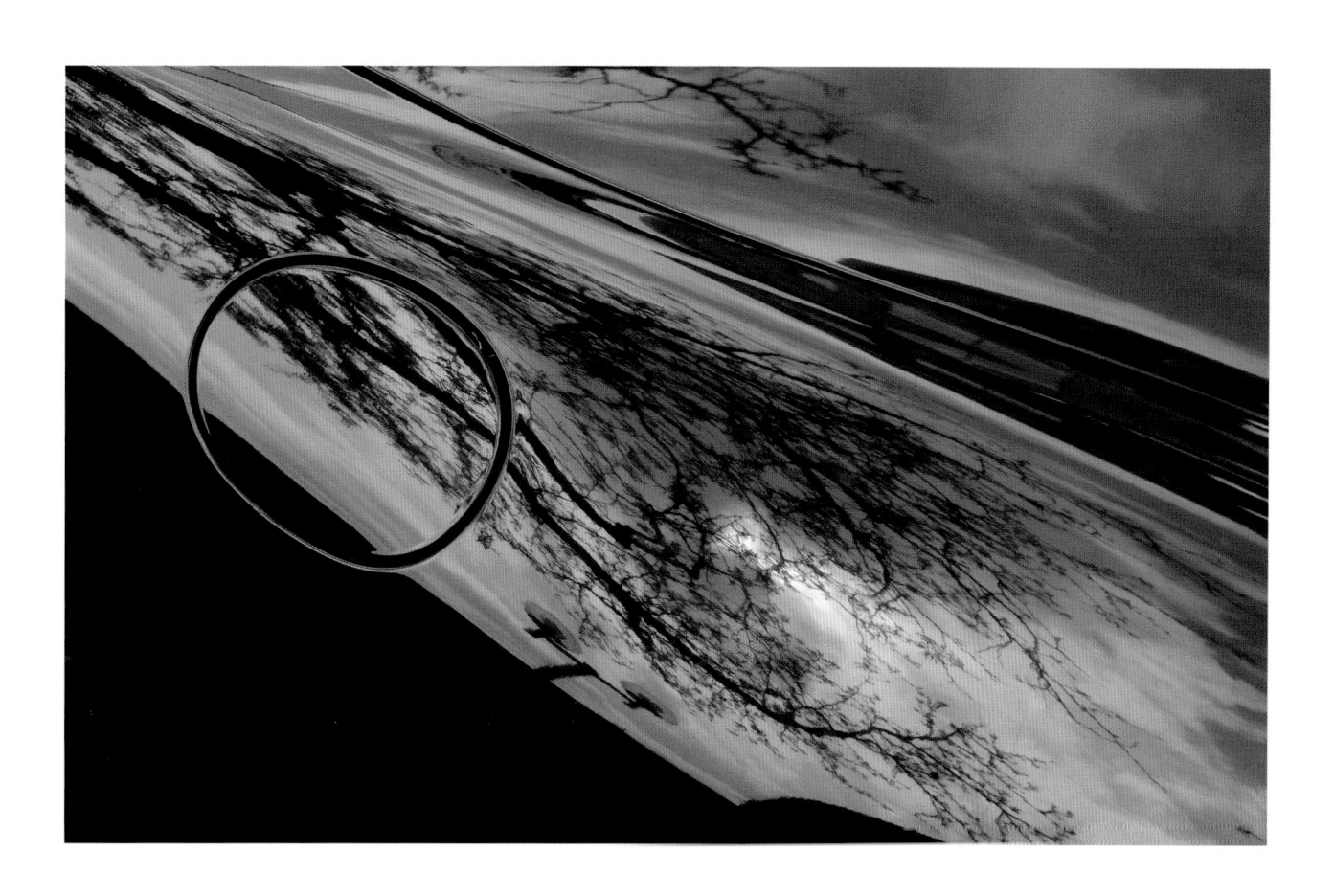

31 EFFORTLESS BEAUTY

TRUE PERCEPTION, TRUE EXPRESSION   32

33   EFFORTLESS BEAUTY

TRUE PERCEPTION, TRUE EXPRESSION 34

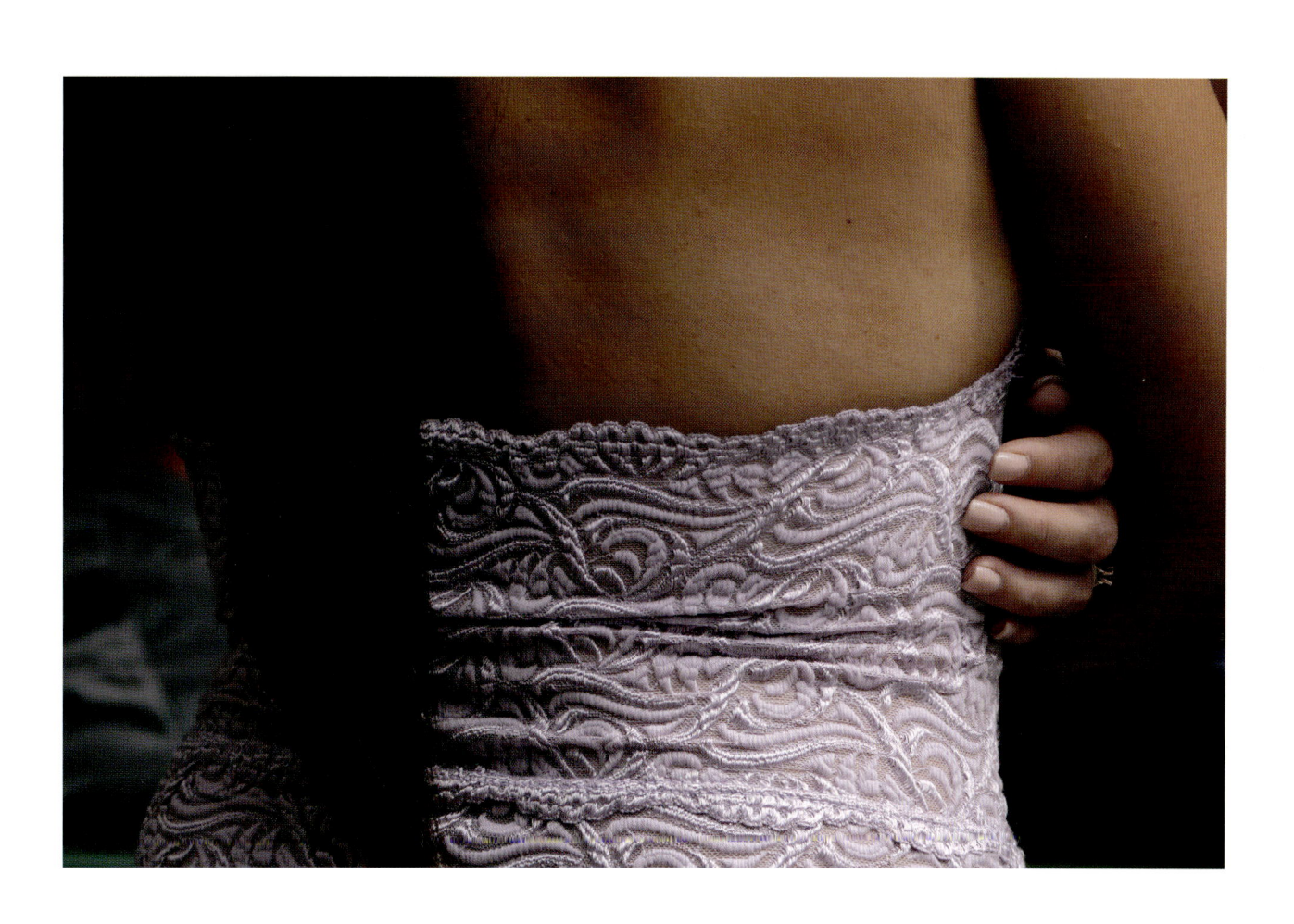

5 Cultivating A Mind of Simplicity

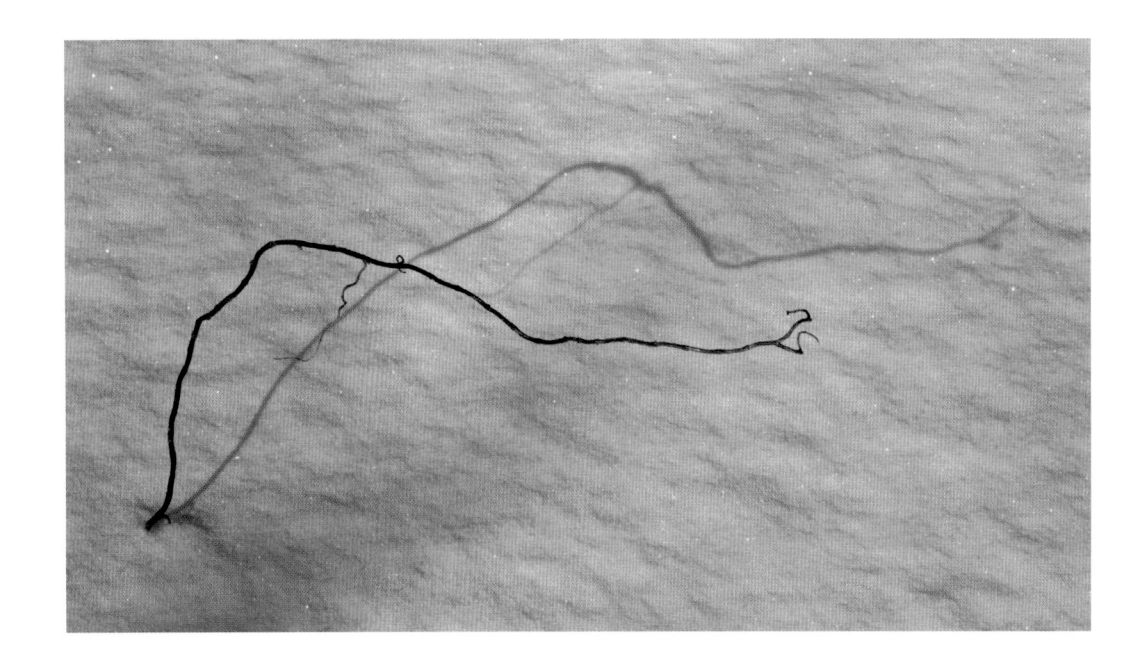

Fully Present, Free from Self Absorption and Distraction

In order to notice our world and see it clearly, we have to simplify our minds. We make a choice to be fully engaged with one thing at one time. This allows us to be fully present in each moment. Of course this simplicity is something that we have to develop. Every thought we have, every impulse we have to move away from stillness, the very restlessness of our minds, resists simplicity. Most of the time we aren't really paying attention to what's going on around us, or even to what we are doing in any given moment. We are lost in thought, our awareness directed inwards as we think about what we had to eat this morning, what we are going to be challenged with at work, whether we have enough food in the fridge to make dinner. Our eye may be seeing, but our mind is distracted. It's like the sound track out of sync with the picture in a movie—lips moving and sound delayed.

We are often disconnected from our experience and we can barely remember what has happened to us. As our life happens to us, we are often not present to experience it.

"Life is what happens to you while you're busy making other plans."
John Lennon

When we think about what we are seeing, in that moment we are not seeing directly, fully. There is an offset in our experience between seeing and thinking. We can learn to repeatedly return our attention to what we are looking at, thereby training ourselves to simplify our minds. It is a discipline that we can work with as we develop the ability to have wonderful perceptions and photograph them.

The beauty of this discipline as a means of training the mind to be fully present is that we see continuously. As long as our eyes are open we are seeing. If we can bring our eye and mind together so that we notice what we are seeing, then it is not possible in that moment for us to be thinking and really seeing at the same time.

37 EFFORTLESS BEAUTY

CULTIVATING A MIND OF SIMPLICITY 38

EFFORTLESS BEAUTY

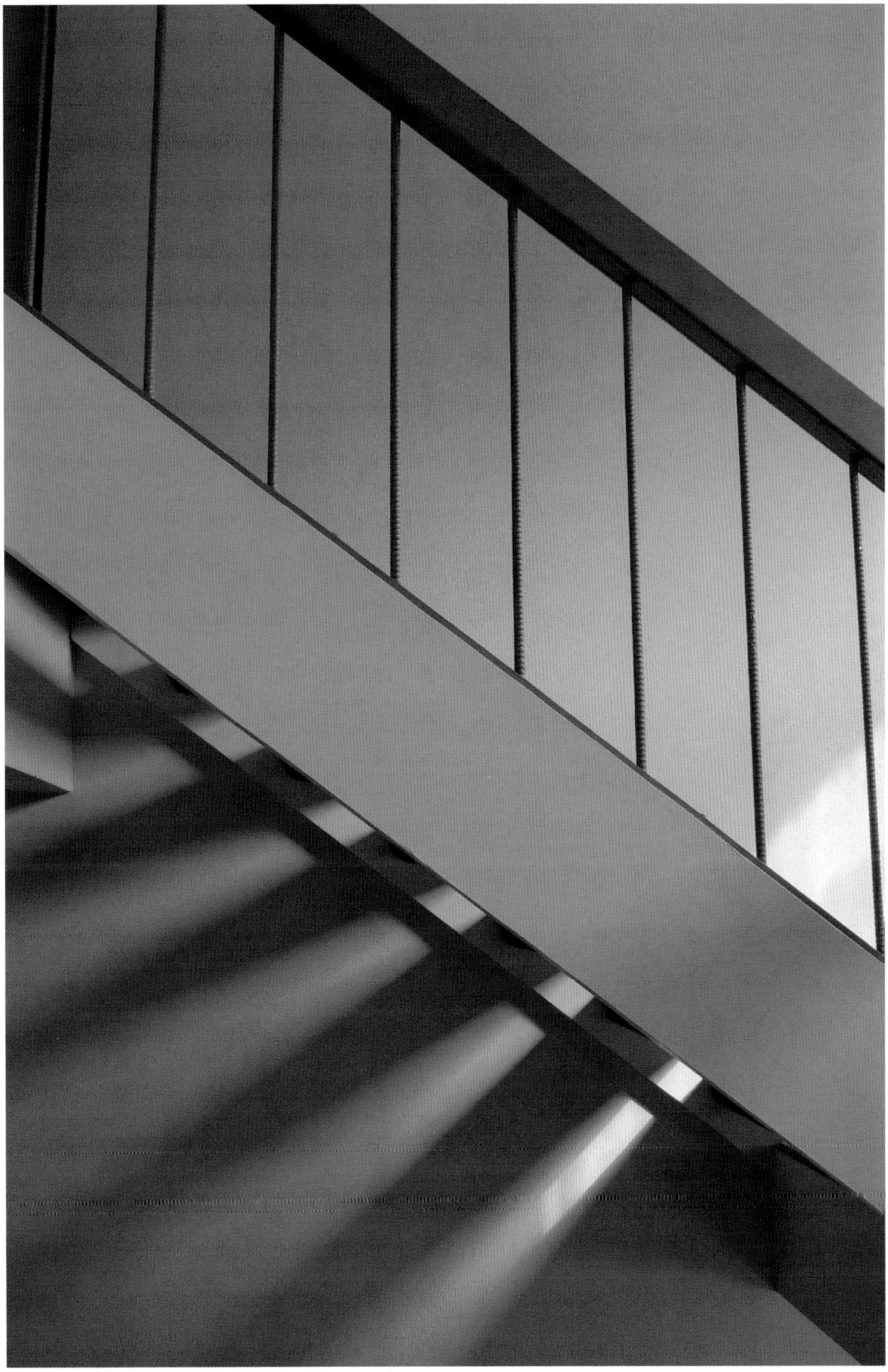

41　EFFORTLESS BEAUTY

CULTIVATING A MIND OF SIMPLICITY   42

6 The Main Ingredients: Stillness and Intention

"In zazen, leave your front door and your back door open. Let thoughts come and go. Just don't serve them tea."

Shunryu Suzuki Roshi

When we allow our thoughts to come and go without becoming involved with them, we find that we can rest our minds in stillness. Our thoughts by their nature are insubstantial and temporary, and if left alone they will float away and lose their cohesion like a cloud in the sky. We do not need to hold on to them. They are a mirage shimmering in the distance as we drive down the highway.

We may feel a pull towards wanting to decide how we like what we see, or a restlessness pushing us towards something else or the next thing. But this impulse to move is only the active nature of our mind trying to kick into gear.

We can just let it be, put in our clutch so to speak, and the engine will settle back into rest mode.

Stillness is an essential ingredient in the ability to see directly. If our mind is fully present and still, and we establish our intention to see, the eye and mind will become unified. The mind and the visual sense join fully through the strength of our intention. Our intention to see is the great activator, and our eye and mind will respond as the intention dictates. Like a lens focusing a beam of light, by focusing our awareness through our visual sense, what we see becomes concentrated, unadulterated, pure, and vivid. Our perceptions will be sudden, shocking, disorienting, brilliant, rich, absorbing, and buoyant.

This is not only a momentary experience. It can be continuous as long as we are able to maintain a steady, direct connection with our perception, unaffected by our distraction. If we can maintain this through to the point we pick up our camera and shift our sight and mind awareness through our camera viewfinder, what we express through the resulting image will have all the directness, the vividness, and the immediacy of the original perception. When we lose track of our intention to see and connect directly with our visual world, the cohesion of eye and mind falls apart and we become uncertain and vague about what we are seeing.

Just as when we tune our radio or television to a particular station, our intention can be shifted to anything on which we would like to focus, any aspect of form or subject matter. We can calibrate our frequency by setting our intention clearly within our mind stream. We can say, "Now I want to see color." "Now I want to see blue, or red," or whatever it may be. "Now I want to see texture". "Now I want to see."

45   EFFORTLESS BEAUTY

THE MAIN INGREDIENTS: STILLNESS AND INTENTION   46

47   EFFORTLESS BEAUTY

THE MAIN INGREDIENTS: STILLNESS AND INTENTION   48

49 EFFORTLESS BEAUTY

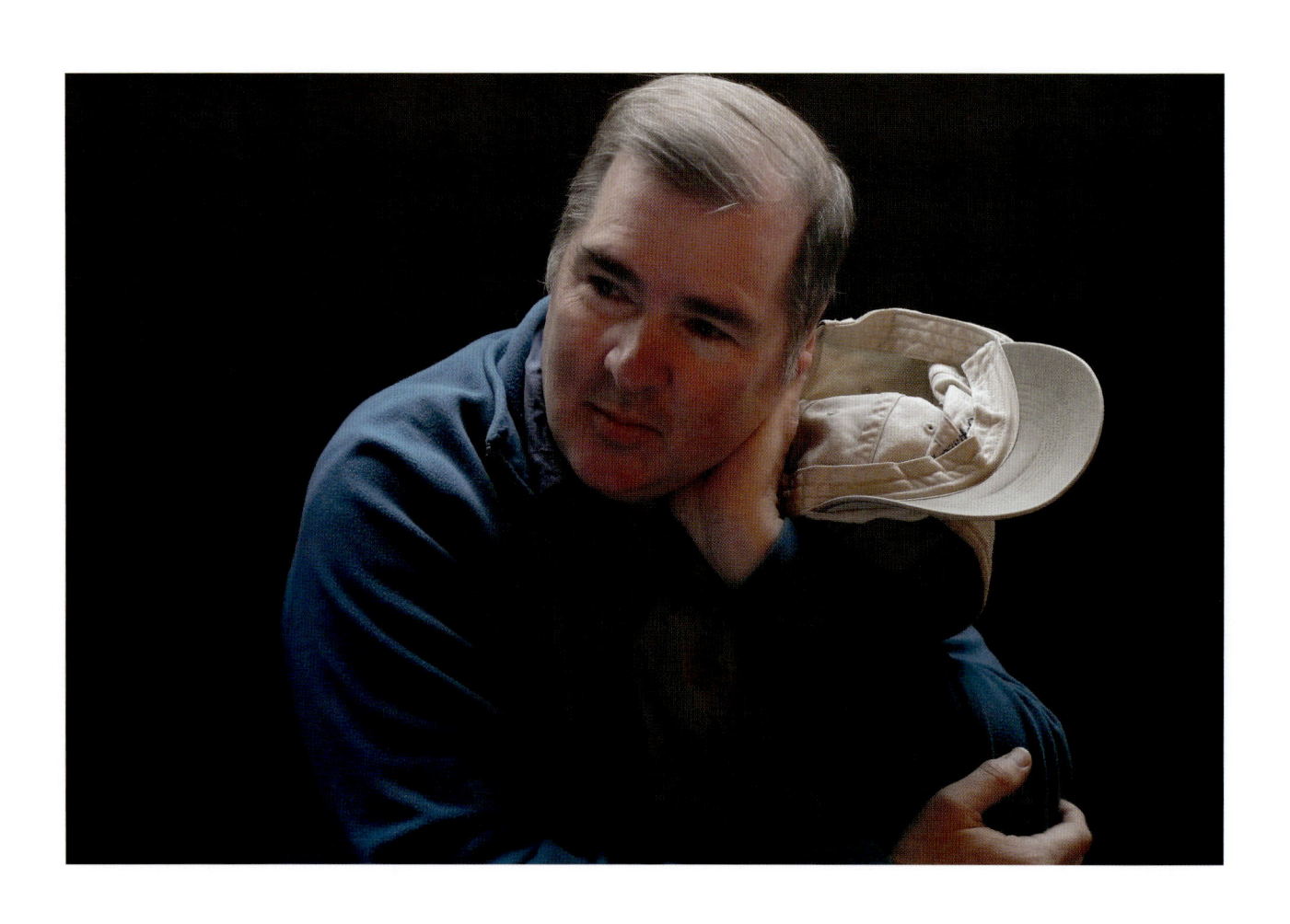

THE MAIN INGREDIENTS: STILLNESS AND INTENTION   50

7   Developing New Sight

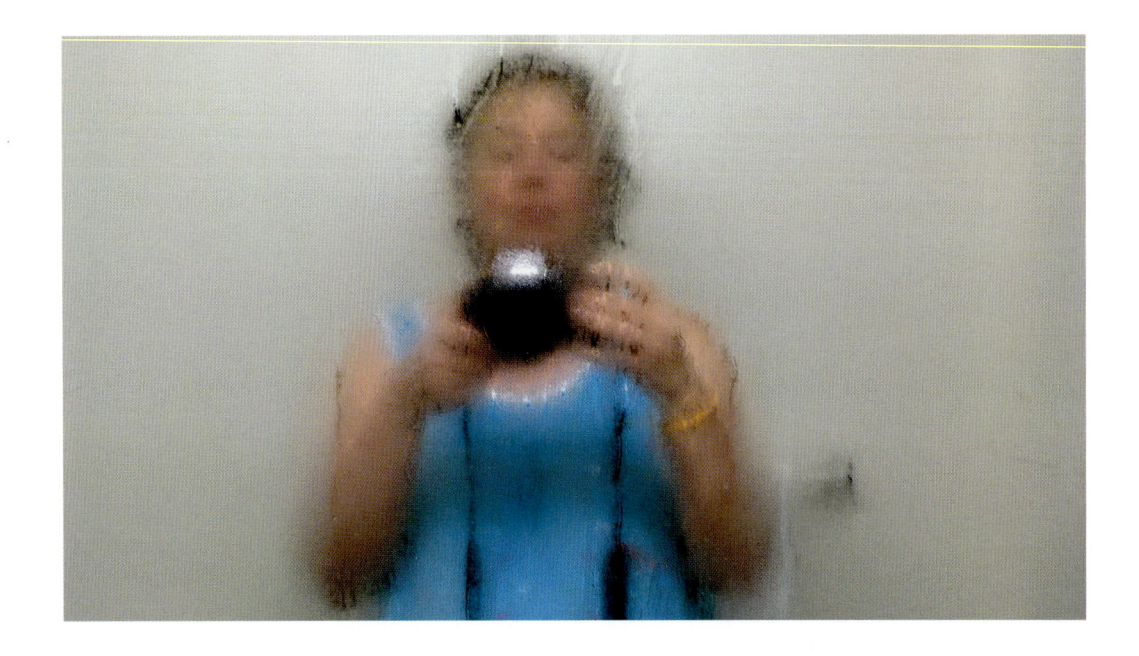

In order to develop our ability to be available, still, and recognize a fresh perception, we begin our practice of simplifying our experience of seeing. We do this by separating out the elements of form and working with each one individually.

Because we learn to be simple in what we see, we begin to develop clarity of intention, clarity about the nature of what we have seen, and clarity about how to express our perception. For example, we could begin with an intention to see only color. Seeing color is a very effective way to synchronize our eye and mind. First we direct our intention to see color and then as we look around, we notice color. As we repeat this, our experience of looking for color becomes more relaxed, more penetrating. Our minds become accustomed to the activity of looking for one thing with one intention for a period of time. Then, as we relax our intention, color begins to spontaneously appear to us. We have looked, applied our discipline of staying steady and directing our awareness outwards to look for color. And as color comes out to meet us, we see.

We repeat this approach with other aspects of form such as texture, light, patterns, and so on. We observe our tendency to immediately label what we are seeing, giving color or texture a name, a context, and putting a spin on it. As we see and start to label what we have seen, we come back to our perception and reestablish our intention. We continue our looking for the form. We abandon content. Form has no meaning. It is just what it is. In this way we train ourselves to see simply, to allow what we see to express itself fully on its own terms. We are preparing to meet our world fully, free of our imposed conditions and preferences.

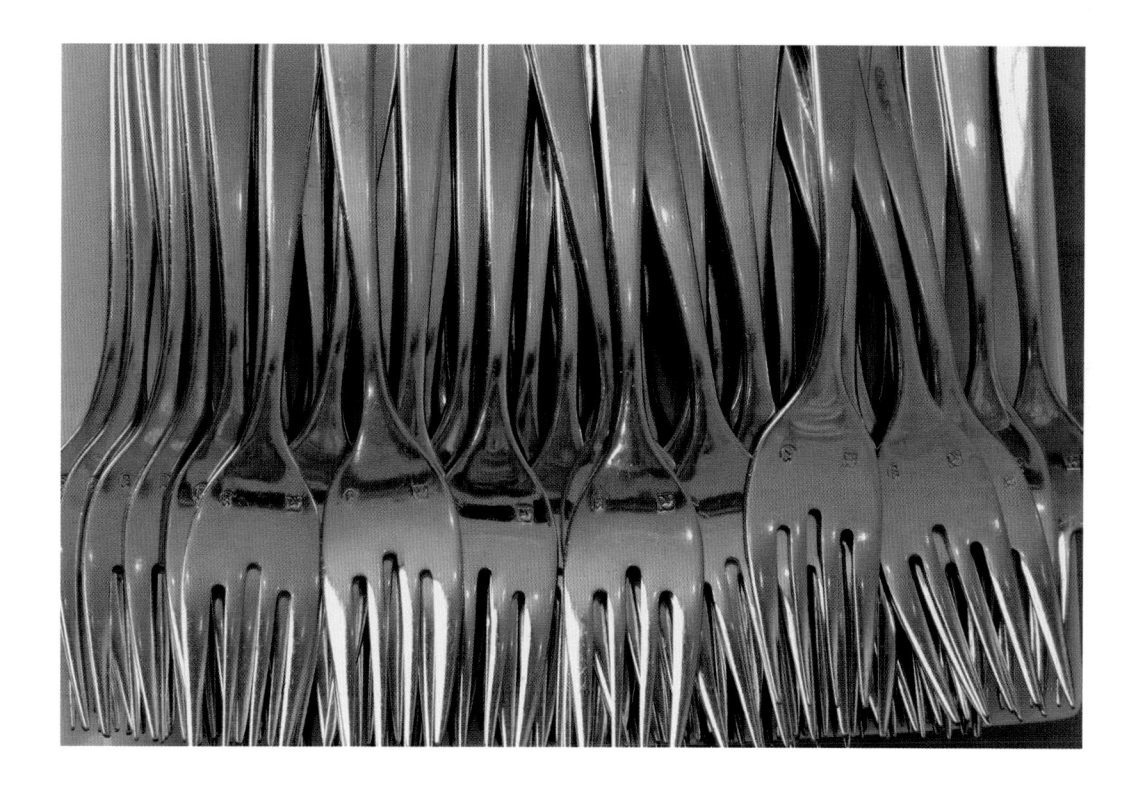

EFFORTLESS BEAUTY

DEVELOPING NEW SIGHT   54

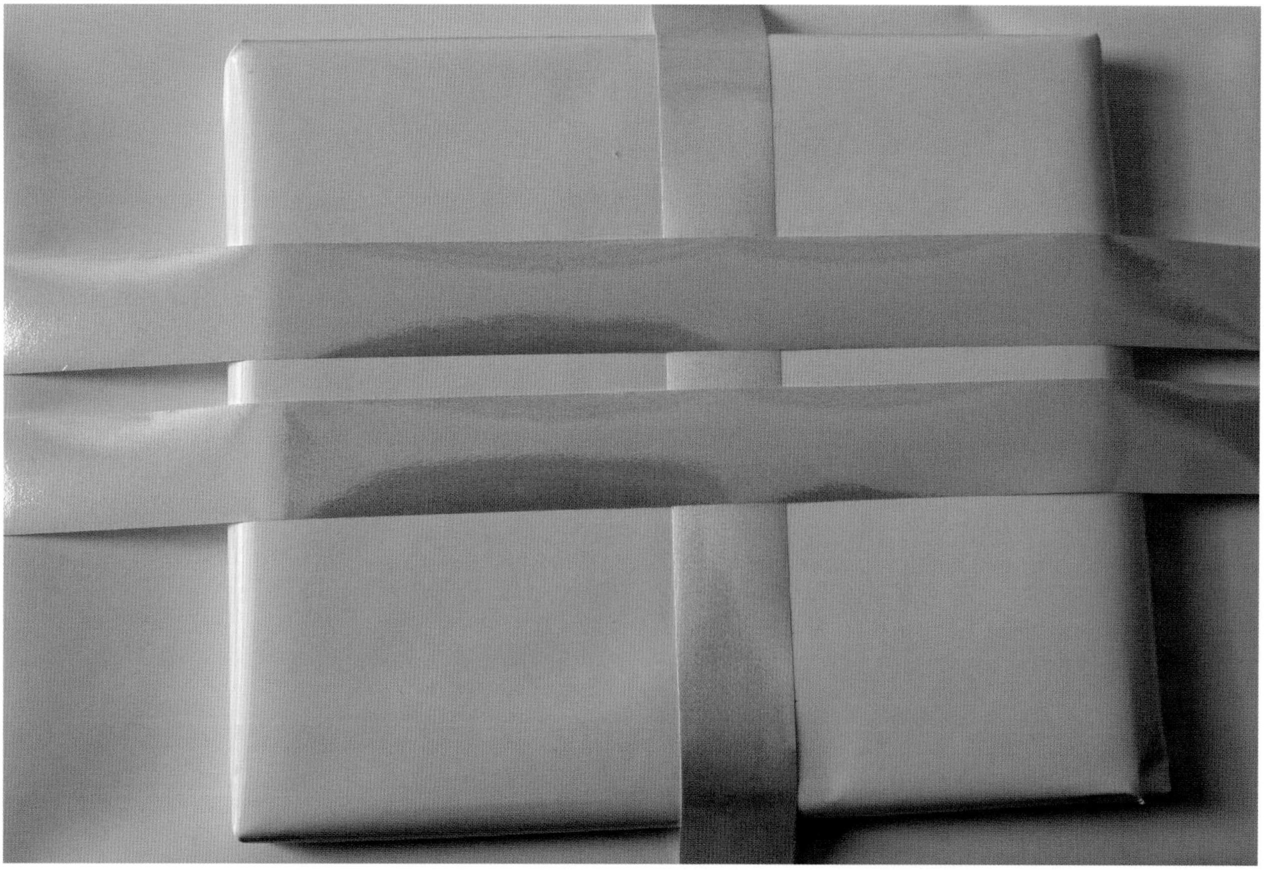

DEVELOPING NEW SIGHT 56

8   Flashes of Lightning

When we are open, available, and our eye and mind are working together as one, we experience our direct perceptions like flashes of lightning in our minds. When lightning flashes in the sky near to us, we can feel the electrical charge in the air as it hovers and then dissipates. Lightning strikes are sudden, shocking, and disorienting. Flashes of direct perception in our minds are just like this.

As we begin this journey of looking and seeing, we find we are able to recognize when we have a flash of direct perception. The qualities of this experience are unmistakable. Our minds are stopped suddenly, abruptly. We are shocked and disoriented, and what we see is vivid, brilliant, and rich. Ambient sounds retreat, and we are filled with a sense of buoyancy. It is right here, in this place where we straddle the world we know and a world we could not have conceived, that the obstacles to direct seeing present themselves.

When we realize that there has been a shift and we find ourselves suspended in a timeless moment beyond our normal experience, we immediately retreat into our familiar world of habitual ways of seeing and classifying our experience. Where are we, what have we seen, is it pleasing, not pleasing, or simply irrelevant? It takes a fraction of a second for us to completely separate ourselves from the direct experience of our perception. The perception has lost its immediacy. It is no longer fresh—it is recycled through our mental content, changed into what we think or feel about it, rather than what it actually is. As we disconnect from the actual experience, we become uncertain about how or what to photograph.

It takes awareness of what is occurring in our minds to stay with the simplicity of that first moment of perception. We can choose to be with it, simply connect to what we have seen, and enjoy it fully without thinking about it, judging, evaluating, or labeling it. A large part of our training in this discipline is to work with this deep impulse to separate ourselves from our experience through labeling and categorizing. We have a tendency to move away from our stillness, to complicate the simplicity of our direct experience. When we learn to be still in our minds as we see, we will maintain our primary connection with the brilliance of our perceptions.

EFFORTLESS BEAUTY

FLASHES OF LIGHTNING 60

EFFORTLESS BEAUTY

FLASHES OF LIGHTNING 62

63   EFFORTLESS BEAUTY

FLASHES OF LIGHTNING   64

9   Coming to a Full Stop

Practically speaking, how does all of this work? We have our intention to see and we are paying attention as our eyes scan through our field of vision. Our mind is relaxed, enjoying the weather, the world around us. It feels good to be out exploring our environment with our camera. Suddenly, we notice that something has connected with our frequency of intention. It is like a homing beacon that has made contact. It stops us dead in our tracks. What has caught our attention? It is time to put on our brakes and come to a full stop. We don't want to miss seeing whatever has shown itself. We have to come to a full stop so we can examine our perception without distraction. Any sense of vagueness about it needs to be clarified through the process of looking further. As we look at what stopped our minds we begin to understand what the perception actually is. Is it the color, the line, the light, the texture, a combination of these? Where does the perception actually begin and where does it end? Is it vertical or horizontal? These questions are primary, for without having the very simple understanding of what stopped us, we are unable to express the exact perception in our photograph.

Understanding in this context is not conceptual. We are not developing a perspective or story line about what we have seen. As we look more deeply, we begin to see. We open further, relax further into our state of seeing, we intimately understand our perception's nature with our whole being—our eye, our mind, and our heart.

Because this process of working with our habitual patterns and dislodging them in order to see is so profound and so basic to how we function, we have to really take our time here. We have to let go of the final step in the process, picking up our camera, and our preoccupation with the final outcome, the image. We have to stay firmly rooted in our open, still state of mind and our perception. With clarity of intention and a still mind, we continue to rest in the nature of the experience of connection that has been established. That perception is the thread of the entire process, from the first moment in which it dawns in our minds through to the experience of viewing it on our computers or on the projector screen. It maintains its freshness because we haven't prepackaged or interpreted it.

Its living quality is always there, just as it was in that first moment. Because of its uncompromised purity and its unstained nature, we could call this a virgin perception. It is unaltered from its original expression in our experience, untainted by our desire to make it our own.

EFFORTLESS BEAUTY

COMING TO A FULL STOP   68

69   EFFORTLESS BEAUTY

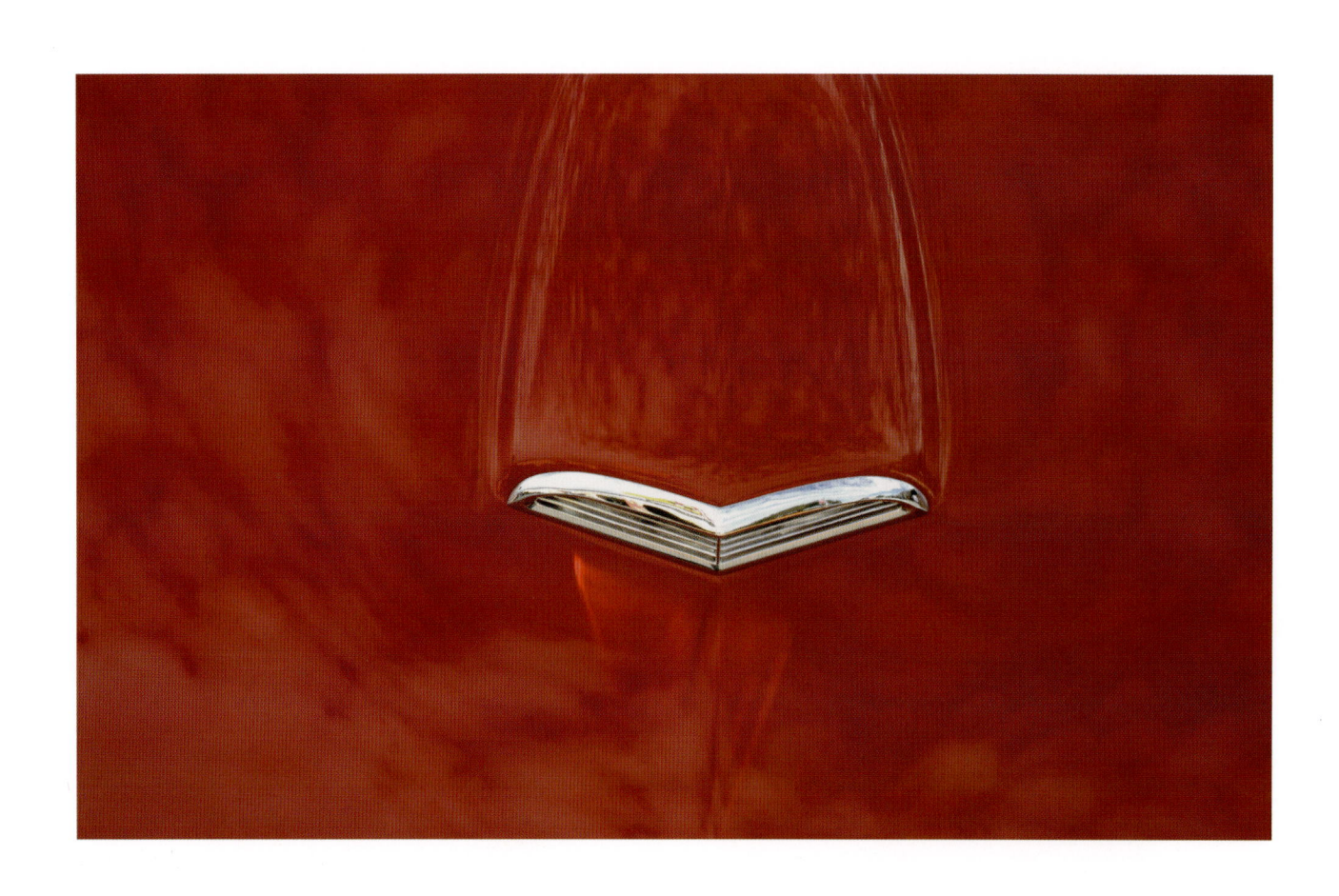

COMING TO A FULL STOP 70

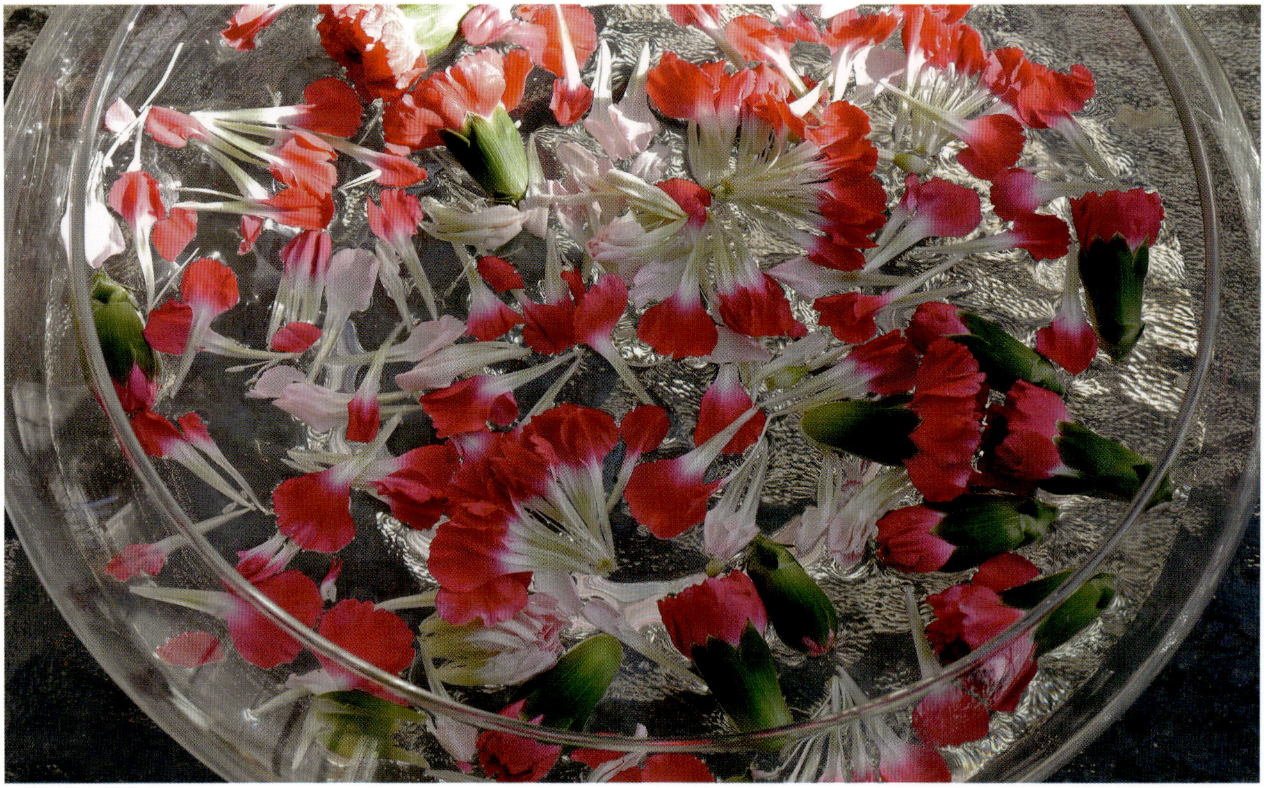

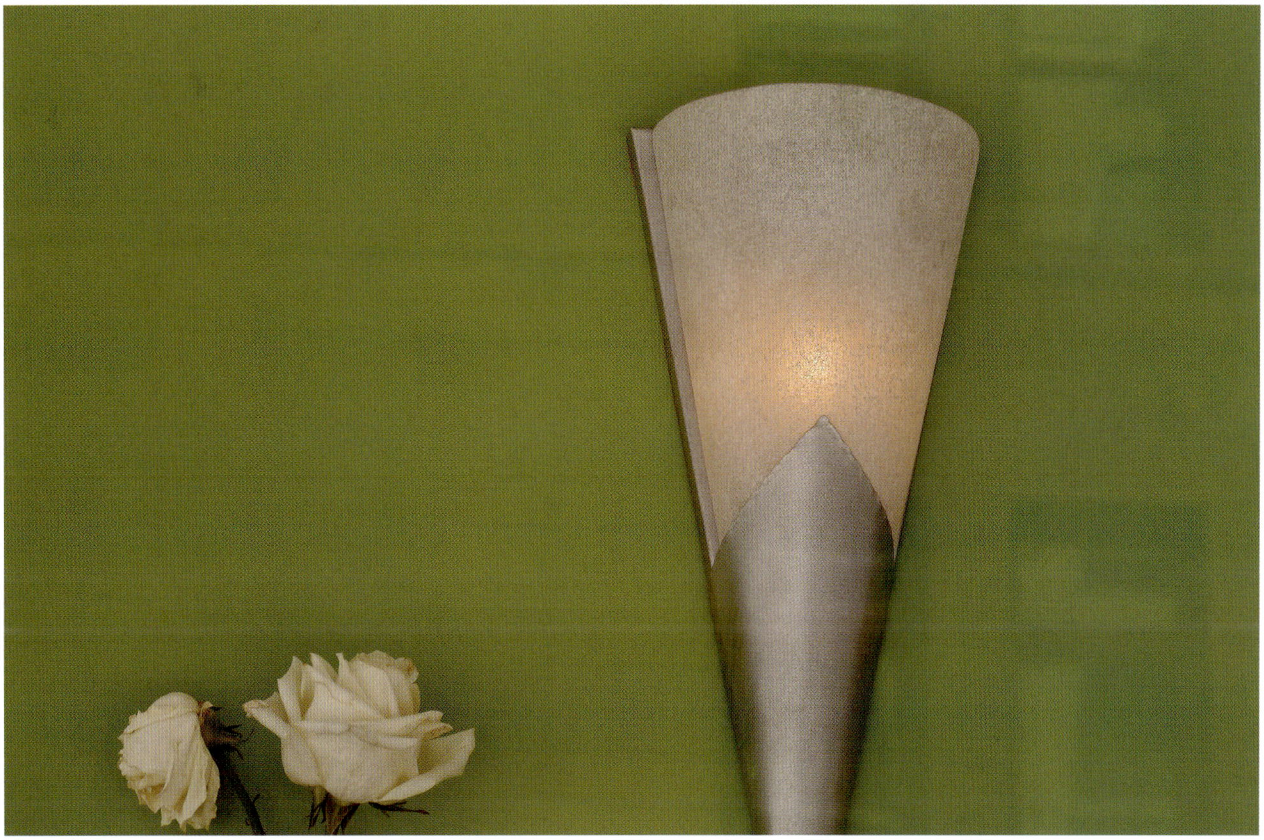

10 Developing Trust in Our Experience

With an open, present mind we see a visual world full of possibilities for connection. With such plentiful, vivid, perceptions, how do we choose what to photograph? If we aren't going to shoot what we think would make an impressive image showing what a good shooter we are, and we aren't going to shoot what we know our friends would recognize as a good photograph, how do we know what to shoot? What is there to photograph?

All of us have moments of panic when we have loosened the grip of our habitual patterns of labeling our experience. It is very disorienting when we don't know what we are looking at. For a split second we don't have any idea about what we are seeing. In this moment we could go either way. We could buy into the labels and judgments that immediately come up in our minds, or we could choose to stay with the openness of not having to know, not having to nail everything down that we experience. It takes time, and lots of practicing the discipline of staying present with the perception, for us to develop certainty that beyond our habitual ways of seeing there are perceptions every bit and more compelling than anything we have ever seen.

This requires some courage to try something really new, and allow ourselves to build our confidence from the experiences that we have with this new approach to perception. We have to look honestly at how we have categorized and labeled our experiences and specifically, our visual experiences, up to now.

It is helpful to understand how those habitual ways of functioning, while being of value in navigating our conventional world (like stopping for a red light, for example), stand between ourselves and the possibility of experiencing our world in a fresh, new way.

It is not unusual for us to doubt the value of our experience, unless it has been confirmed and validated by others. We are also taught that unless something has significance it isn't worthy of notice. But we're not even sure what that means, that everything has to mean something. Imputed meaning is completely relative—it is always changing and being reinterpreted according to changing views. In the midst of uncertainty we look to experts, those who claim certainty about their point of view, to tell us what our experience signifies or doesn't, what is of value. We need them to provide clarity and context and relieve our anxiety. That corroboration brings a sense of hollow confidence that isn't really based on anything grounded in our own experience. In the world of direct perception, perception without our usual reference points, our final image becomes our only external confirmation of our inner experience. It is all we have, and if the photograph remains true to our perception, then every one will experience what we have seen.

Doubt about the value of our perception can, and sometimes does, arise because without applying our usual filters and preferences to our experience, we are simply open and groundless.

We aren't flashing our identity card. This brings exhilaration and insecurity at the same time. If we can stay connected with the thread of the perception in spite of our not knowing conceptually how it fits or what it might mean, then we can produce a photograph that expresses the depth and dimensionality of our experience.

75 EFFORTLESS BEAUTY

DEVELOPING TRUST IN OUR EXPERIENCE   76

77   EFFORTLESS BEAUTY

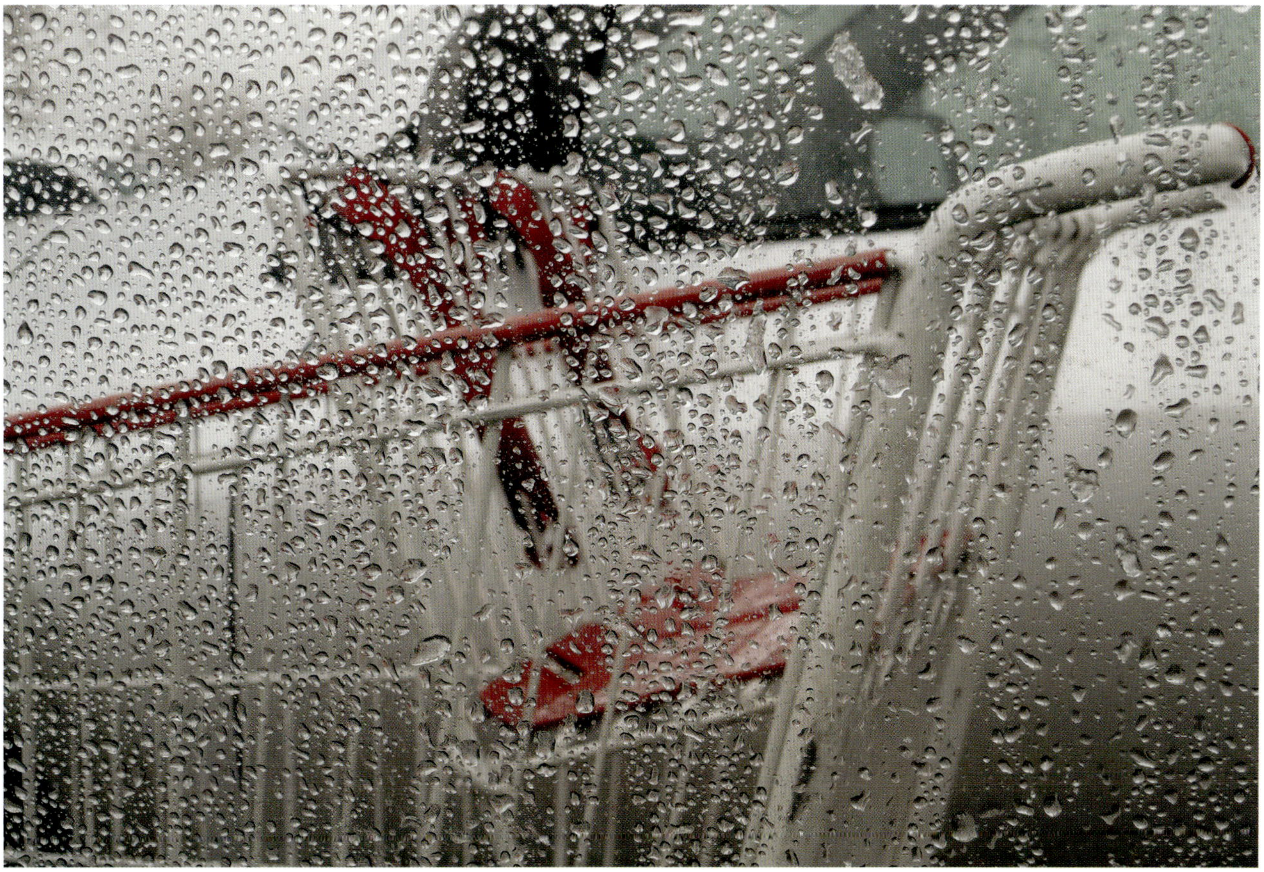

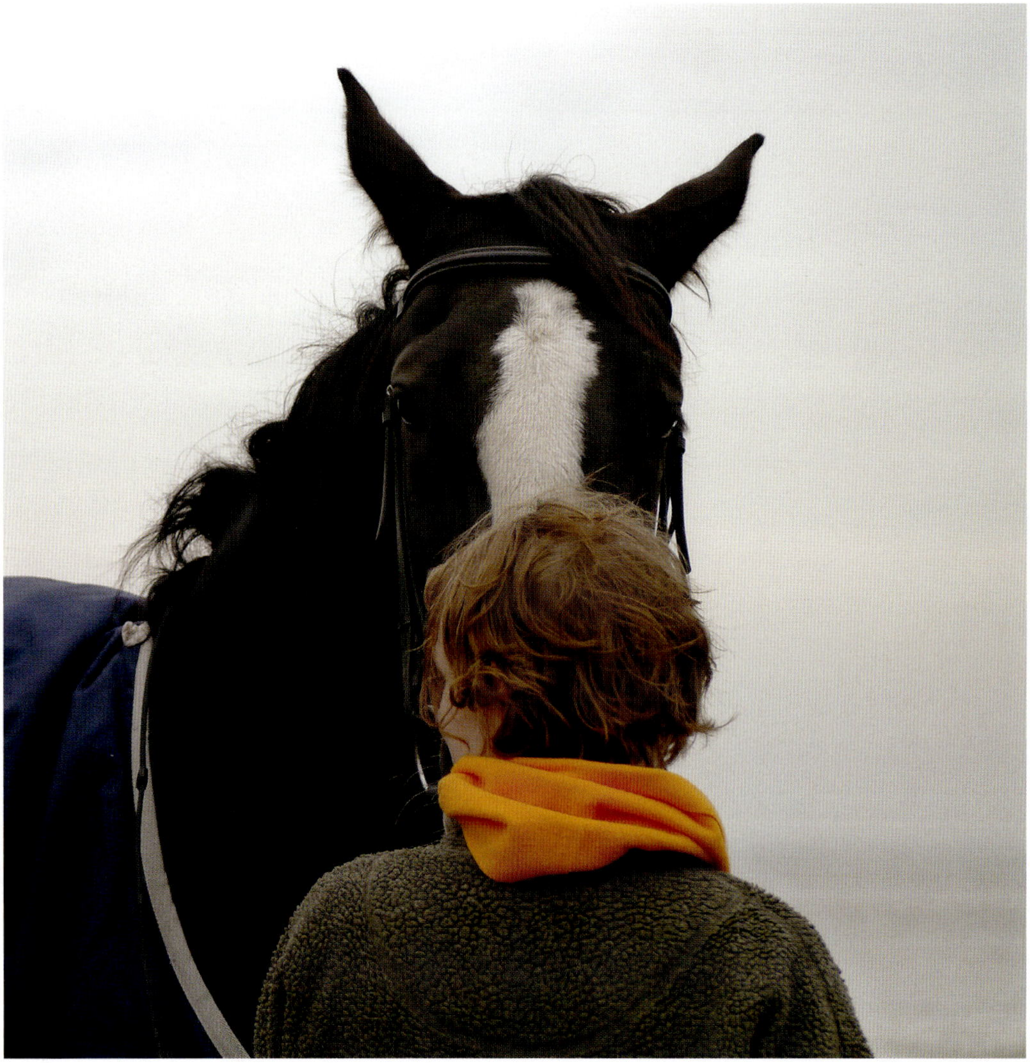

DEVELOPING TRUST IN OUR EXPERIENCE 80

11 Resting Fully in Our Perception

We have been stopped suddenly, abruptly, and we have dropped out of warp speed, coming to a full stop in front of our perception. We settle down and hang out, relaxing with our new perception, simply looking at it and taking it in. As we continue to rest in stillness with what we have seen, we notice more deeply the details, the hues, the contours, light, and shadow, the feeling tone of our perception. We begin to feel it penetrating us so that we can feel it under our skin. We don't want our attention to wander so that we lose this moment of meeting. It has not come about accidentally. It has happened because we made ourselves available and in this particular place and time, this unique perception has come forth to meet us. It is this deep noticing that allows us to translate our experience into an image that expresses fully the qualities of this meeting. We do not want to be haphazard or rushed.

It is as though we just met someone by chance and we are completely amazed at our good fortune. It is like love at first sight. We are here, they are here, we are both noticing the world around us, and then we see each other. If it had been a different time and place, we may not have ever seen each other. Without feeling self-conscious, we come forward to extend ourselves, to become acquainted. We look at each other. We smile. We exchange simple words and, feeling attracted, we move closer. As we allow ourselves to open further, we feel our senses filled, almost intoxicated with the experience of this person. Sounds become distant and the only thing we see or hear is our new acquaintance. We are absorbed. Our hearts feel the bottom fall out. We begin to feel like we could melt into this person. Everything about them is perfect. This experience has imprinted itself indelibly upon us. We know we will always remember it.

EFFORTLESS BEAUTY

RESTING FULLY IN OUR PERCEPTION   84

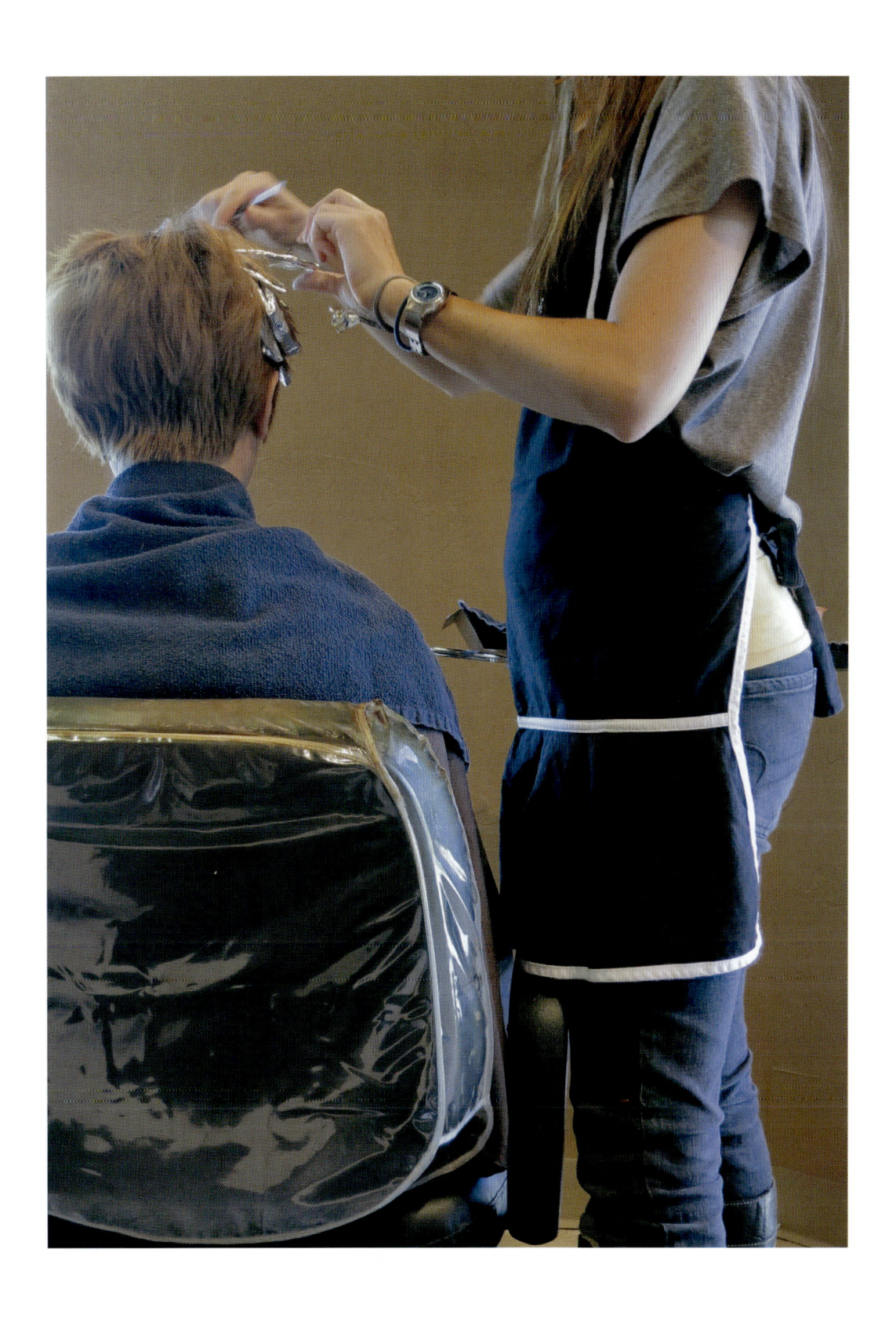

EFFORTLESS BEAUTY

RESTING FULLY IN OUR PERCEPTION   86

87 EFFORTLESS BEAUTY

RESTING FULLY IN OUR PERCEPTION   88

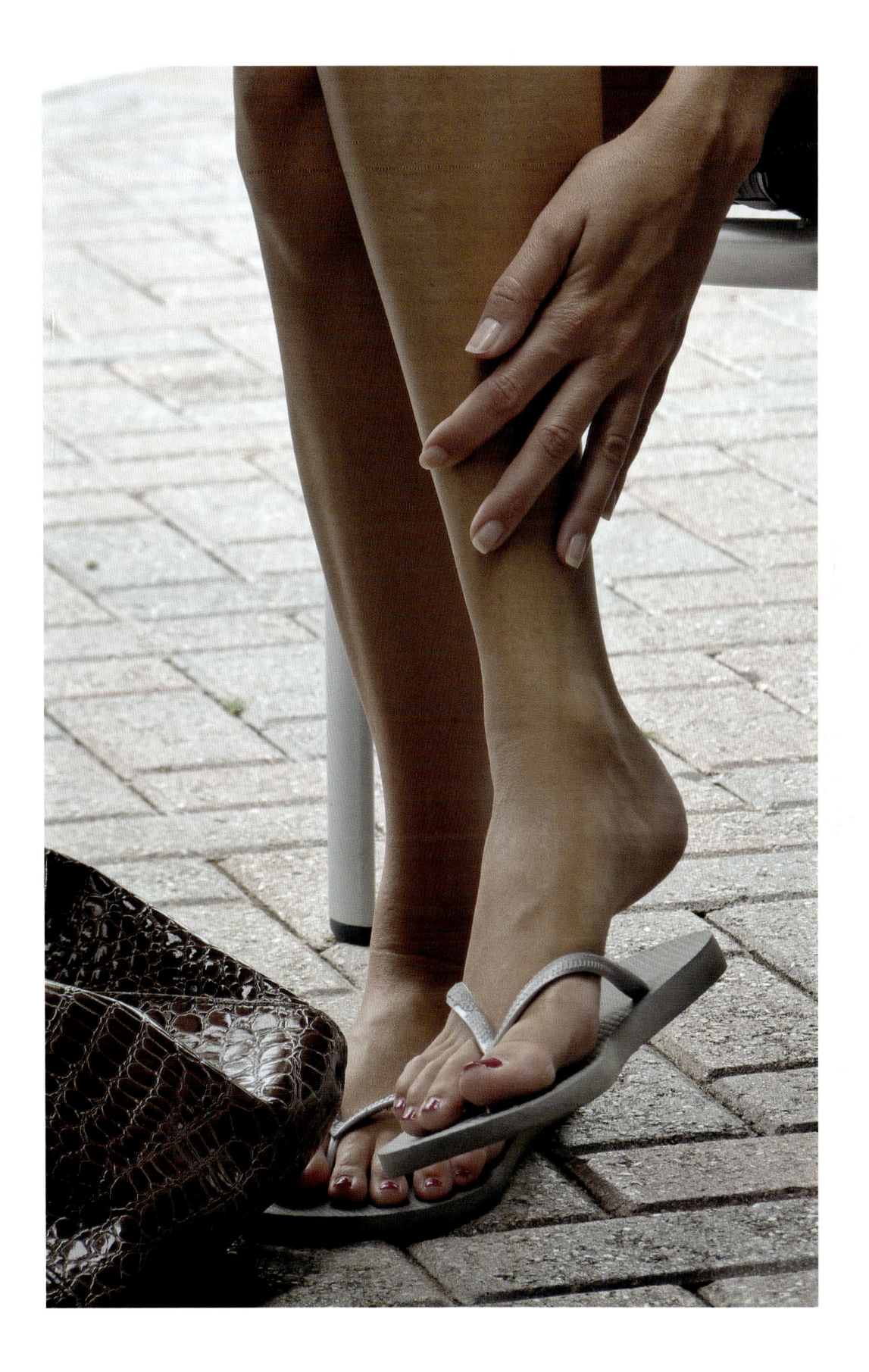

12 The Image as Completion

When we have had a perception that we feel this way about, we don't have to say goodbye. We can commit to this experience of relationship by making an image of it with our camera.

We have all the time we need. At this point we begin to carefully consider how we will express our experience. What depth of field should we use? What is in focus and out of focus? How light or dark is the perception? Where should we take our exposure? Once we determine what is needed we then, and only then, bring our camera to our eye. Then there is one final question. Is anything added or missing? Is this exactly what my perception is? Then if the answer is yes, we squeeze the shutter. Squeezing the shutter is the consummation of the relationship.

As we bring the camera back down to our side, we once again appreciate what we have seen. This is full commitment. And because we have rested in stillness, appreciated our experience fully, and we have paid very close attention to all of its aspects, we will know what adjustments need to be made in our editing to bring the image to express exactly the color, light, quality of the perception. We will know in our body and in our mind. We will resonate with it when it is right. It is like tuning a guitar. When the strings resonate in unison, in perfect alignment harmonically, there is only one sound. It is just right.

Sometimes when we try to see directly with our eye, mind, and heart, questions come up. Why take a photograph? Why not just have the experience of the perception and let that be enough in itself? Perhaps because we have a deep need to share our experience. And in the process of taking the photograph exactly as we have seen it, we transform the perception from something that we remember into a living expression of our experience.

Because our relationship with this perception is so full-bodied, because we have connected with our mind and our heart, we can come back to the image of this perception again and again and experience the freshness of that first moment. We have honored our experience of perception fully. This process uplifts our minds and brings us deep contentment in being alive in our world.

EFFORTLESS BEAUTY

THE IMAGE AS COMPLETION 92

93　EFFORTLESS BEAUTY

THE IMAGE AS COMPLETION

13   Unwound and Relaxed

I love Sunday mornings. I wake up early enough, but not too early. The first thing I notice is how quiet it is outside my windows. The endless stream of cars heading to their destinations has ceased. I realize that I do not have to put my daily regimen into gear. I can put in the clutch and coast for a while. I can move at my own pace, free of external influence, and let the day unwind in a natural rhythm. I feel a tremendous sense of relief, together with a basic sense of wellbeing and contentedness.

Because I have noticed and appreciated the stillness of the Sunday morning, I can allow myself to open out into a world of possibility. There is room for me to take my time and examine my choices for what I do, and when I do it, and choose according to what I want. Instead of the usual relentless sense of trying to be somewhere and do something, I have room to breathe, to renew myself, and refresh my being. This sense of freedom is a wonderful feeling. On Sundays for me it arises out of the recognition and appreciation of stillness. When we slow down, unwind, and just be, we can have a quiet mind.

There is all the room we need to relax and enjoy ourselves. In this space of openness, all things are possible.

We are all familiar with the eerie calm of nature before a storm. All is quiet as the birds stop their sounds. The wind becomes very still. There is a sense of waiting for something to begin, an electrical impulse hanging in the air. When lightning strikes, the stillness abruptly transforms into an eruption of light, sound, and energized movement. It is like this for us when we experience direct perception.

As we relax and expand our mind into our environment, we are prepared to engage. We are relaxed, curious, paying attention, and passionate about connecting fully to anything that meets us. We are fully primed to see, waiting, and yet very still inside. As our mind's eye is noticing what is around us, we are not thinking about anything. Inside we do not move. We see, we notice, but our mind does not move. Then, out of nowhere, a perception erupts. We are fully met in that instant. A new relationship has begun.

When we set out with our camera to explore the world, we begin from stillness. We have to start from somewhere. Having a still mind is the way in. In a practical way, we have to turn our antenna to the sky. This antenna is stillness.

How do we rest our mind in stillness? We can allow ourselves to breathe out, release our worries, our daily concerns. We can let our mind expand out and rest there. Stillness can accommodate all of it. There is lots of room. We can let our thoughts come and go and who cares? We don't have to hold onto them or make them more than they are, simple thoughts. We are preparing to meet our visual world. We feel fresh because we don't have an agenda, nothing particular to see or do. We can set out to wander anywhere we feel like going, take our time, and digest thoroughly what we see.

Sometimes it is difficult to find our stillness. I find it very helpful to fully stop moving and stand still in one place. Then I feel my feet on the ground. I shift my awareness to my body and how it feels to me. As I breathe out, I let the tension I am holding in my shoulders go. I notice any tension in my head, my arms, my back, and then I let go of all of it as I exhale slowly and completely from my head to my feet.

I do three long out-breaths and in-breaths as I sink into an awareness of my body. Then I raise my gaze and look out without particularly focusing on anything, and rest there, until I begin thinking about what I am seeing.

As soon as I notice that my mental engines have begun to shift into first gear and that I am labeling what I am seeing such as mailbox, road sign, and so on, I gently close my eyes. I let go of my thoughts about what I have seen. I let all of it dissolve. And as I do, I bring my attention back to my body, standing here, on the ground. I breathe a few times. I feel the goodness of being here in this moment. Then I turn a half turn. I hang there, between what I just saw, and what I will see. And when I am fully resting in that place between the past and the future, with no thoughts about the present moment, I gently open my eyes again. If a label or thought arises, I simply close my eyes and let it all dissolve. This exercise is very relaxing, very grounding. And by doing it we start to feel like we don't have to go anywhere or do anything. We are resting in stillness.

Sometimes it is difficult to settle our minds, to unwind. This is not a problem. When my mind is overwhelmed by my thoughts, I am very gentle with myself.

Becoming grounded in my body through feeling its sensations and paying relaxed attention to the sounds, the temperature, the air, the simplicity of just being, feels very natural. It is a relief to settle down onto the earth. We can just hang out and be patient with ourselves. We can take all the time we need. Each time our mind gets caught up in thinking, we simply come back again and again to our body and our senses.

We can do this short stillness practice wherever we are, in a café, in our living room, on a train. Because connecting with our stillness is not dependant upon something or someone outside of ourselves, it is always a possibility for us, wherever we are. As we become more familiar with the experience of stillness and how simple it is to rest in it, we develop confidence in our stability and strength. We can bring ourselves into stillness whenever we choose.

UNWOUND AND RELAXED   98

EFFORTLESS BEAUTY

UNWOUND AND RELAXED 100

101 EFFORTLESS BEAUTY

UNWOUND AND RELAXED 102

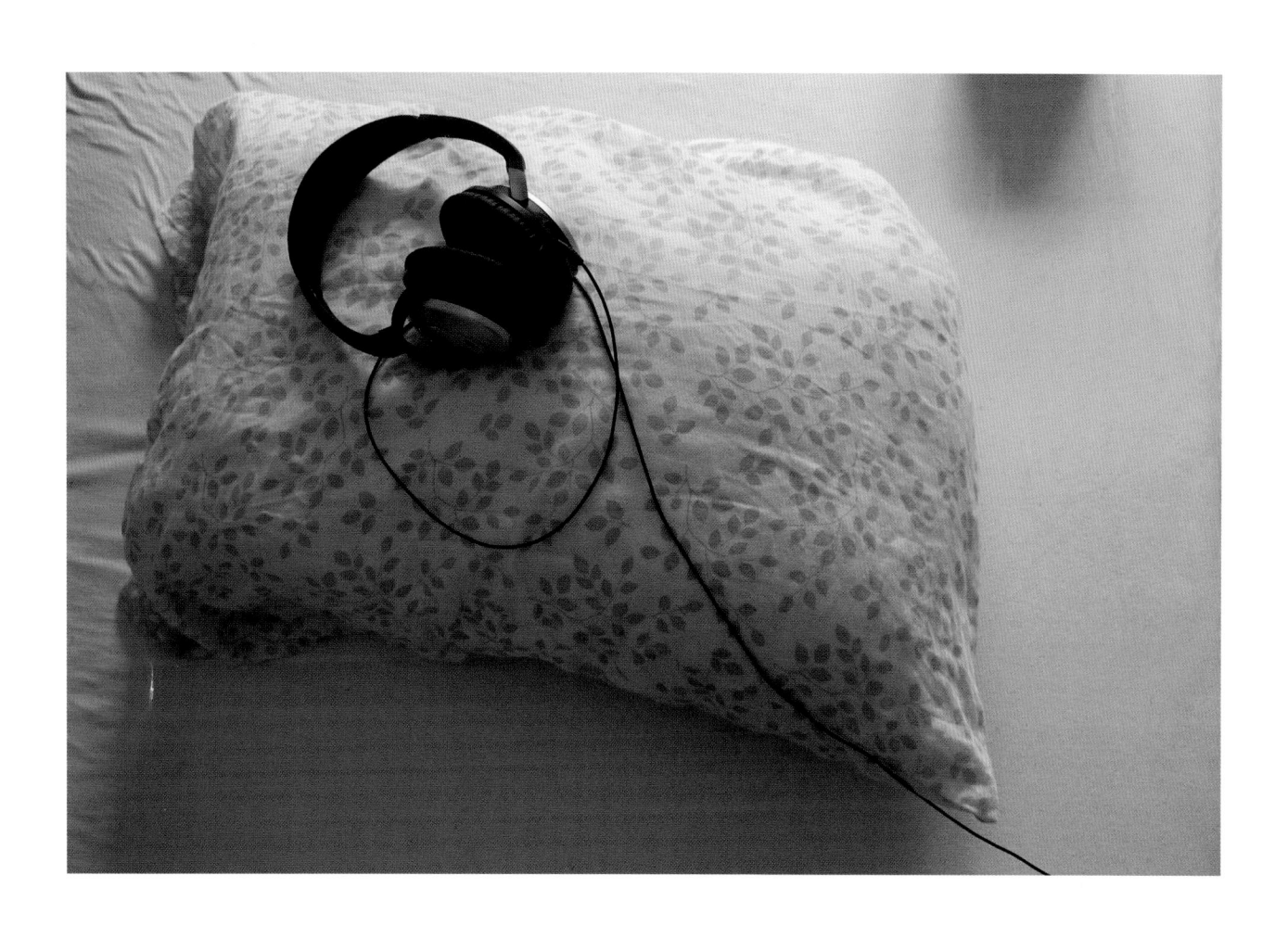

The Pause that Refreshes

The thread of stillness is a river of relaxed continuity that is the basis of our experience of direct seeing and photographing our perception. Without stillness there is no possibility for us to be in a state of openness, availability, and absence of agenda that is essential for us to connect unconditionally with what we see. This fundamental stillness does not mean that motion ceases, that we stop what we are doing. It can mean that we are not the primary reference point, constantly checking in to see what we think or how we can refer back to a moment that has just passed. It means that we rest our minds fully in the present moment. Whenever we feel the impulse to push ahead, to move to the next phase in the process of taking a photograph of what we have seen, we can let go, relax into our stillness, and rest our minds there.

Because we return over and over to stillness, we continuously refresh. This means that all movement towards expression of our perception is firmly rooted in the first experience of direct seeing, not based on an impulse, which was based upon another impulse, leading us away from our primary experience. Keeping each aspect of our experience and its expression totally fresh brings a tremendous sense of directness and immediacy to our images.

In this way, not one single thought can make its way into the expression of our perception. When our mind wanders to who said what to us and what that might mean, we can bring ourselves back to stillness. When we wonder if what we saw would make two different photographs, we come back to stillness. It is like hitting a refresh button over and over, each time coming back to balance and openness, keeping us firmly rooted in our genuineness. We do not have to create what is not there. We can absorb what we are seeing through our pores and let any hiccups in our experience dissolve into a full-bodied sense of what is there. And all this while our mind does not wander.

Stillness is the great equalizer, keeping us free of hoping for better, for more, for success, and fearing that we may not measure up or be good enough. Because of our allegiance to our genuineness, our expression of our visual perception is sealed with stillness and freshness. As we come back again and again and rest the mind in stillness, we find that holding on to our personal point of view becomes less interesting to us. As it loses its grip on us, we begin to feel a shift of allegiance in our being from holding on to letting go.

Working to maintain our worldview every second can seem like we are trying to hold on to sand. There is nothing solid that we can hold onto. Our world is not for or against us. Our so-called solid point of view is full of gaps, and space and openness. The drive to impose conformity or context upon our experience begins to seem like a pointless expenditure of energy. We begin to feel our grip on our view of the world relaxing. It is not this or that, good, or bad, depressing or exciting. This is equanimity. Our mind is steady in stillness.

We feel good and the world is a profoundly interesting place to be. This equanimity brings confidence and certainty that such a thing as unconditional perception and expression is possible.

We are ready to make a leap further into having an unconditional relationship with our visual world. We want to experience the world fully as it is.

105   EFFORTLESS BEAUTY

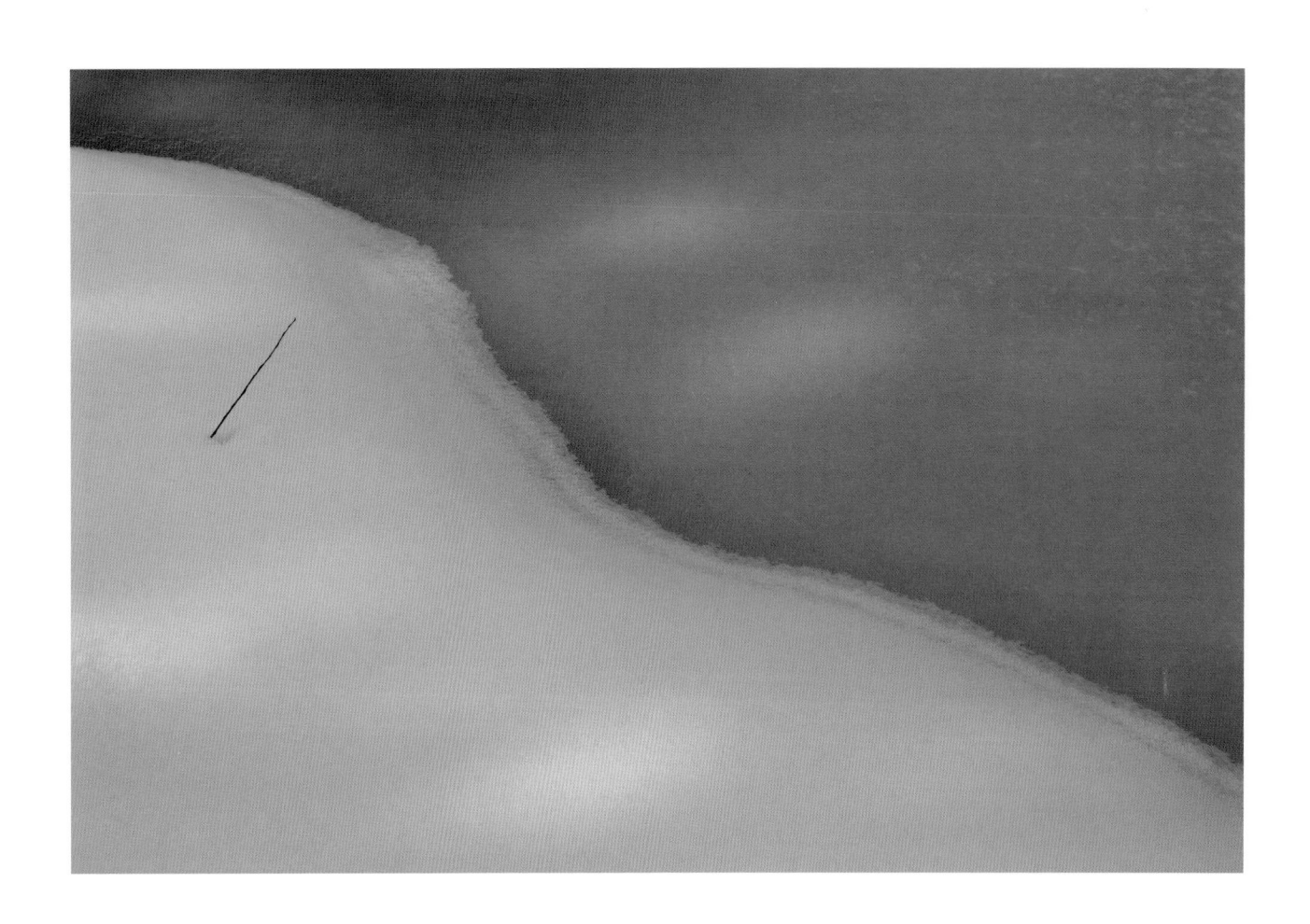

UNWOUND AND RELAXED   106

EFFORTLESS BEAUTY

UNWOUND AND RELAXED   108

14 Intimate Seeing: Engaging the Body and Mind

Every one of us is a completely unique combination of elements. What we share is that we are human. We have a human body, a human heart, and when we are truly open and available, we have the capacity to experience sense perceptions that we never imagined. We all have sensors far beyond our physical body: when we walk into a room, down a street, or into a store, if we are paying attention we can immediately feel the quality of that place. We sense it. As with all of our senses, what we feel in the space attracts us, repulses us, or leaves us indifferent. One thing is for sure. Seeing does not only happen in our eyes. It registers in our body experience as well. Our mind and our body function together as a unit. We are not always aware of this aspect of seeing. Many photographers feel most comfortable as observers and feel a degree of security in this unengaged status. They are comfortable in the realm of ideas, of thoughts, precision of thinking. The body can be messy. Emotions get sticky. But when the mind is still, the body can be still as well. We can allow its sensations to be, just as

EFFORTLESS BEAUTY

we can be open and available to our world without prejudice. Then as we are still, we begin to notice the expression of our body's sensation of seeing.

Seeing is an experience of both the mind and the body. We are not concerned with the particulars of our body. We don't have to think about it. We can feel its sensation. It is not separate from our mind. Body and mind are like a hand in a glove. Our glove is our body and our mind is the hand, which fits our glove perfectly. They are a match made in heaven. In this human life, they are inseparable. We don't have to regard our body and all the sensations associated with it as an obstacle to direct seeing. When our mind is still, we can be still in our body.

As we are still, we can relax and breathe. We can feel the wind on our skin and blowing through our hair. We can feel the sunlight on our face. When we feel sensation, we take it in like a sponge. We absorb it and process it internally, very quickly. If we pay attention we can feel it. This is as much a part of our experience of seeing as our experience in our mind. If we can pay attention to this aspect of perception, we can become fully absorbed in the experience we are having. So when we are stopped by a perception, we physically stop. When we are fully inside a perception, we are aware of how our body feels as we see, appreciate, and resonate with what we are seeing. It is a complete experience. Seeing completely brings us down to earth. We can connect with the water-ness of water, the hardness of stone, and the roughness of rock.

When we are still in both our body and mind, we can be unmoving. This is the only moment we have, right now. Any impulse to jump after something we think will be good or that excites us, any perception that fits into our database of really cool images, doesn't move us. We can just let it be.

Our stillness is the basic ground of direct seeing. It is the deepest and most innate situation. Because we have the intention to see, we have a willingness to remain in that stillness and not jump after everything that arises in our mind/body. As we take in our world, we take it in deeply.

As Zen Master Dogen said:

*"Seeing forms with the whole body and mind—
One understands them intimately."*

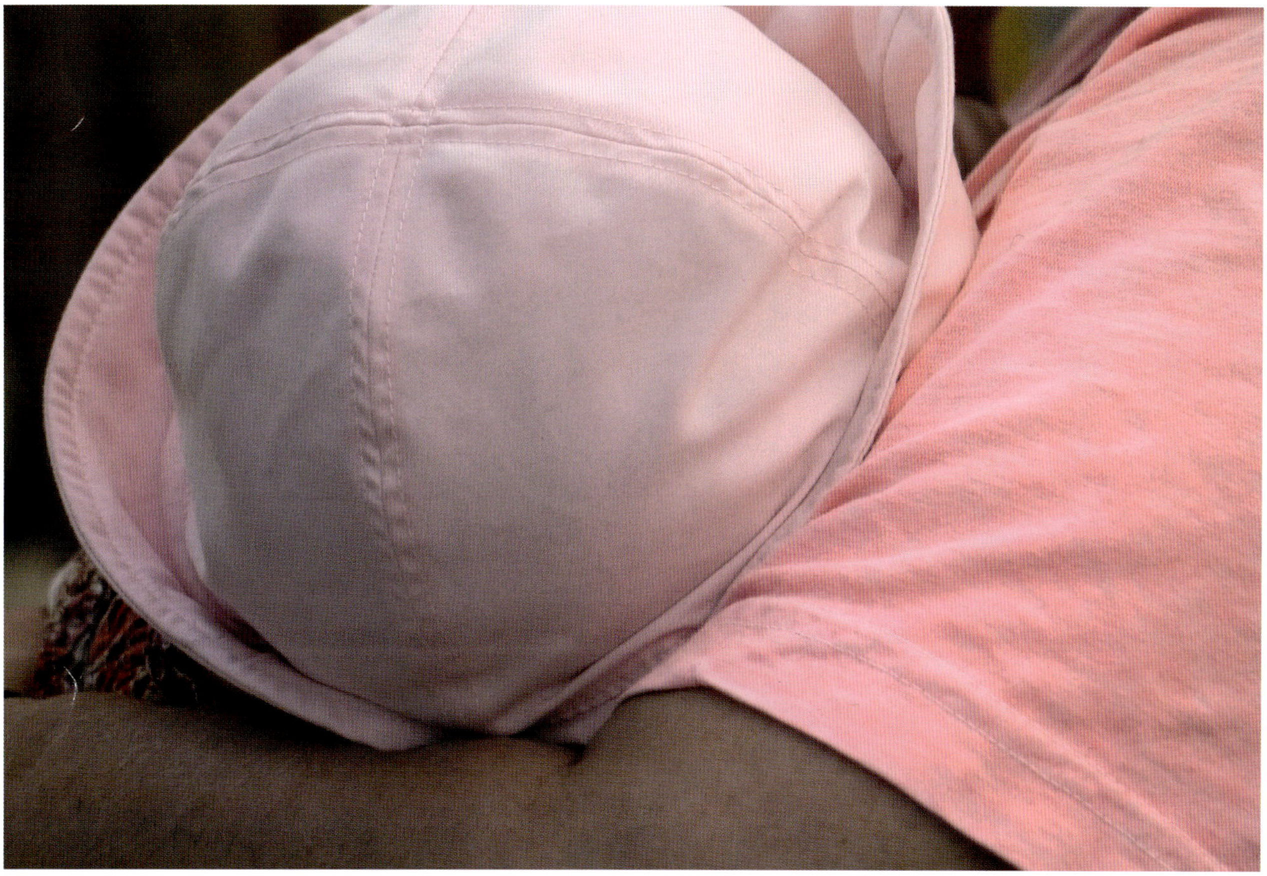

113   EFFORTLESS BEAUTY

INTIMATE SEEING: ENGAGING THE BODY AND MIND

15   The Gateway to Perception: Dissolving Boredom

When we begin our journey into the world of direct seeing it is all new and challenging. We are surprised at how easily, with the help of visual exercises and some guidance from a skillful teacher, we can connect with our visual world. But as we continue to apply ourselves to the assignments we are given, the freshness of our previous experience is difficult to find. We have ideas about what we should be seeing. We would like our images to be as successful as before, but what was fresh yesterday is today's old news. It can seem like no matter how hard we look, we don't see anything we want to photograph.

We find ourselves wondering if we couldn't be doing something more useful and exciting with our time. Fortunately, because of yesterday's success, we are willing to hang in there with our resistance. We have come up against our boredom. Our mind is restless. We are not satisfied. We want to be somewhere else, in a different moment, in a different place.

Our external barometer of satisfaction is registering pretty low, and alarms are sounding in our heads. The possibility of escape comes to mind.

During all this preoccupation with our state of mind, we miss out on what is happening right where we are. We cannot experience our experience because we are unable to settle down and rest in a mind of stillness.

We have many thoughts about our dissatisfaction, but they are just like any other thoughts we have. They have no substance, no solidity. We have not yet fully realized that to see freshly there is no alternative besides letting go of our expectations.

There is no other way into direct perception than to move through our boredom. If we strategize about how to add "interesting elements" or images that we "like", we are avoiding the basic point.

To connect with the situation as it is, to have the experience of direct seeing, we have to let go. No matter how much we feel limited by what we think is there for us to see, we have to let go of our ideas in order to enter into a direct relationship with seeing our world. Finally, at some point, we exhaust ourselves. We let go completely of what we want to see, our ideas of what makes a worthwhile experience.

This letting go is the active intention, the active principle, which allows us to open out and to be still so that we can perceive more deeply. Without letting go we can't be still, because even if we want to stand there and look at our perception, our minds are still producing thoughts, still perceiving, still thinking about what has been perceived, still deciding whether it is good, bad, ugly, whatever.

Through our intention to see, we turn our awareness outwards, we make ourselves available. Then our intention to let go of what stands between us and seeing is activated. We let the thoughts come and go without disturbing our equanimity. The intention to let go is the basis of the effort in this practice. It keeps us rooted in an open, fully present state of mind. We let go into right now.

As we let go, our awareness expands out into our environment. Our mind rests in the experience of openness and evenness. In this space of accommodation, we feel gentle, peaceful. As we have traveled through the gate of boredom, we have moved into a realm of direct perception. Inside this realm, time is standing still. We float through it noticing and appreciating all the elements, the aspects, the smoothness, the roughness, and the natural elegance. Our mind of evenness, equanimity, stillness keeps us steady. As we appreciate and touch, we feel that we are insubstantial, light as air, empty of the reference point of me and my personal investment in this activity. Our perceptions present themselves as they are, on their own terms. We discover that we are being penetrated by them, in our mind and in our body. This is the full-bodied experience of visual perception.

Making direct contact with our world is where we experience the blood and guts of direct perception. We have no idea, we are blindsided by the intensity and totality of what has stopped us. Whatever it is, it has presented itself as a big red stop sign. GO NO FURTHER! NOWHERE TO GO BUT RIGHT HERE! We are riveted—we are glued. There are no holes in our connection, nowhere for our eye to wander. We have made contact.

THE GATEWAY TO PERCEPTION: DISSOLVING BOREDOM   118

EFFORTLESS BEAUTY

THE GATEWAY TO PERCEPTION: DISSOLVING BOREDOM   120

121 EFFORTLESS BEAUTY

THE GATEWAY TO PERCEPTION: DISSOLVING BOREDOM   122

16   Making Contact

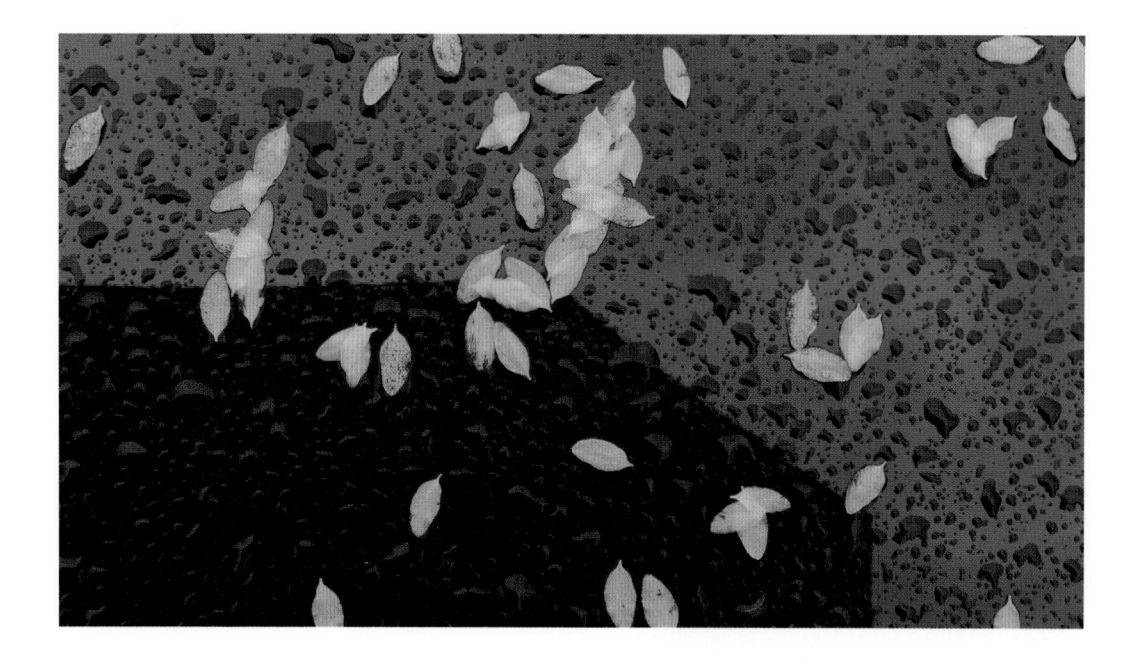

If we have genuinely applied ourselves to our practice of visually conscious seeing, then we have discovered that there are limitless perceptions available to us to photograph. We do not ever need to fear that our perception is the only one or best one we will see; we don't need to feel that if we can't express our perception, we have failed and we are disappointed. We can keep our minds open, return to the open state of possibility and in a very short time, we will once again be stopped by a brilliant, vivid perception. To remind ourselves that we do not have to feel a sense of poverty and desperation, we say, "There are limitless perceptions." If we can remember this, we will always be able to start fresh. We will be able to abandon a perception that we cannot express, or that we have to struggle to understand. Our practice of seeing will be joyful and unencumbered by hope and fear. As our visual awareness becomes steady, we find we can go out looking with an increased stability of stillness. We may have thoughts come up, we always do. But our attention is not placed on the thoughts. With discipline and exertion, we have trained ourselves to stay alert in the present moment.

Thinking happens very quickly and we can get absorbed in thought before we realize what is happening. But then, because of our passion to see and because the joy of direct perception has become our primary motivation, our discipline kicks in and jerks us back to what is happening in the present moment. We let go, and come back to where we are and start fresh. Each moment is a fresh beginning.

The driving force in direct seeing is inquisitiveness. Our attentive mind possesses tremendous curiosity to investigate, to engage with, and to understand our world. We want to contact and connect with what we are seeing. We want to feel it, understand its qualities, and then we want to photograph it. We can suspend our personal agenda, our credentials. When thoughts arise in our mind, we can let them be.

Our continuity of connection with our perceptions becomes longer and deeper than the flashes of perception we have experienced previously. Without our familiar conceptual framework tethering us to our habitual ways of seeing and understanding what we see, we begin to feel like we are floating through a floating world.

There is a simple practice that we can do that can allow us to experience the shift in awareness from looking for the highlights in our visual world to a state of deep noticing. To begin, we need the intention to be open and to relax into a mind of inquisitiveness. It is helpful to establish a time for our practice session and to stick with it, not allowing ourselves an exit option when we become restless and bored. Fifteen minutes could be a good minimum amount of time. It would be helpful to have a flexible lens that could zoom out to 90mm and which includes macro.

We find a place to sit down, in a spot that we choose, where we can stay unmoving and undistracted as we look at a defined area. It could be in our home, our backyard, on a park bench. It could be anywhere. As we sit, we simply look, and as fresh perceptions come to us, we photograph them. We don't move around or get up to change position, regardless of how restless or bored we may feel. We stay seated and simply look.

In the beginning, typically we notice the highlights of what we are seeing, the visually obvious. As we photograph, we feel a sense of satisfaction that these images will be successful, admired, and everyone will recognize them as great perceptions. After a time, after we have plucked the low-lying apples from the tree, we may begin to think that we have seen everything that is there. We have looked and looked, and we are getting tired of looking. In fact, we wonder why we allotted fifteen minutes for this exercise. But we remember our intention and determine to stay the course. We squirm and shift our weight on our seat. Then we exhale and look again.

To our surprise, we notice something we hadn't seen before, and then more. It is like we have begun seeing a new, fresh scene. It is a new beginning. It is at this point, when we have exhausted the sense that there may be something more interesting taking place 'over there', that real seeing takes place. Sailors refer to this as a 'sea change', when the ocean tides change direction entirely.

This change of direction can only occur and be noticed when we are still, open, and unmoving. In terms of our visual life, this is the most profound moment there is. We let go of what we want to see and suddenly see what is there.

We become entranced, gently moving our mind's eye throughout the scene, touching gently with our eye what comes forward to be seen. We notice new subtleties of tonality, shape, line, shadow, light, color. We find that we have become very still, and very engaged at the same time. We feel open, still, and unmoving, inquisitive and curious, passionate, disciplined, and deliberate, and we feel well seated. We are in a state of deep noticing. We feel ourselves floating together with what we see. Seeing in this way is a process of unfolding, veils dissolving so the quality of what we are seeing starts to manifest.

As we transcend boredom, we can fully experience our world.

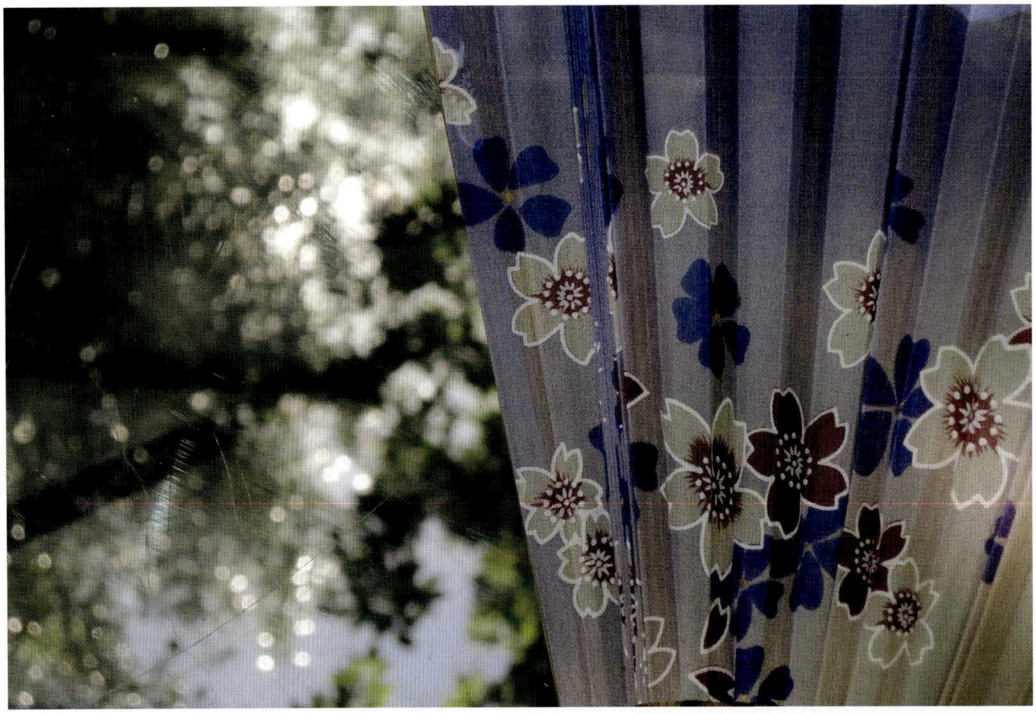

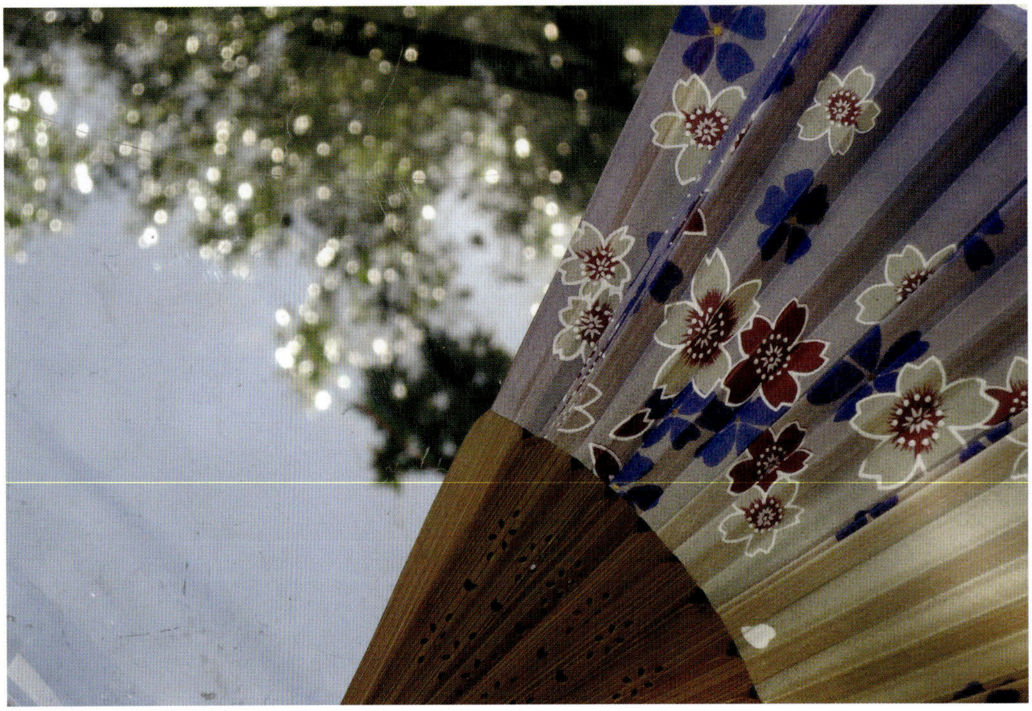

MAKING CONTACT 128

129   EFFORTLESS BEAUTY

MAKING CONTACT   130

131   EFFORTLESS BEAUTY

MAKING CONTACT 132

17   Exploring Fields of Perception

Sometimes when I am not particularly paying attention to anything, my eye and mind can be stopped by a visual perception. This perception is abrupt and sudden, interrupting my mental content. It stops my mind. There are other times when I am really in the zone, nothing really happening in my mind. I am very relaxed and present, scanning the environment, feeling where I am. Within this state of not much happening in my mind, something can simply manifest. It is something appearing out of nothing. It is a surprise, a deep pleasure. This is what we sometimes call exploring within a Field of Perception. That Field of Perception is wherever we are in the present moment.

It could be that the Boulder Mall is a Field of Perception. I am walking around with my camera, exploring and open to being gently magnetized by a situation taking place. It could be some people playing their instruments, or a busker performing. It could be light illuminating the pavement or an alleyway. These are all within the Field called the Boulder Pedestrian Mall.

EXPLORING FIELDS OF PERCEPTION   134

EFFORTLESS BEAUTY

We have a small pond near our house. It has water, trees, reflections, texture it has it all. This is the Field of Perception of our neighborhood pond. It has many elements and qualities, changing constantly moment to moment. Each hour of the day, every shift in light, weather, season, brings new visual wonders.

When we first begin working with this approach to seeing directly, when we are stopped by a perception, we experience the sudden, abrupt cessation of all thought as we realize we have made a connection. As our discipline and confidence become strengthened, we begin to experience the river of stillness as the continuity of our perceptions. We are increasingly able to stay steady and undistracted as we understand, appreciate, and express our perception. When our minds are resting in stillness, the contrast between seeing and not seeing is less apparent. The quality of being stopped becomes less abrupt, as the contrast between not seeing and seeing becomes less sharp. We no longer are very distracted and suddenly completely present with our perception. We are more present all of the time, especially when we are fully engaged in looking and seeing, and so the experience of seeing is more continuous and gentle. We are pulled towards the perception like metal to a magnet.

Our entire being is part of the perception, and we are part of the fabric of the place, the environment. Within this sense of wholeness we are drawn in more deeply. As we take in our perception, we experience a sense of seamless resonance. We experience our perception as an integral part of the context of its environment. When we are exploring a field of perception, part of understanding our perception is to experience its totality, its "That-ness." It is not separate and individual. It arises out of, and from within, the Field of Perception.

Making contact with water is one of the greatest of all experiences. I love to swim. When I hit the water, in that first second, I gasp as I am completely overwhelmed by the sensation of cold wetness. It is a total experience, a single moment in which my thinking mind is completely off-line. I experience the "That-ness" of water. Water-ness.

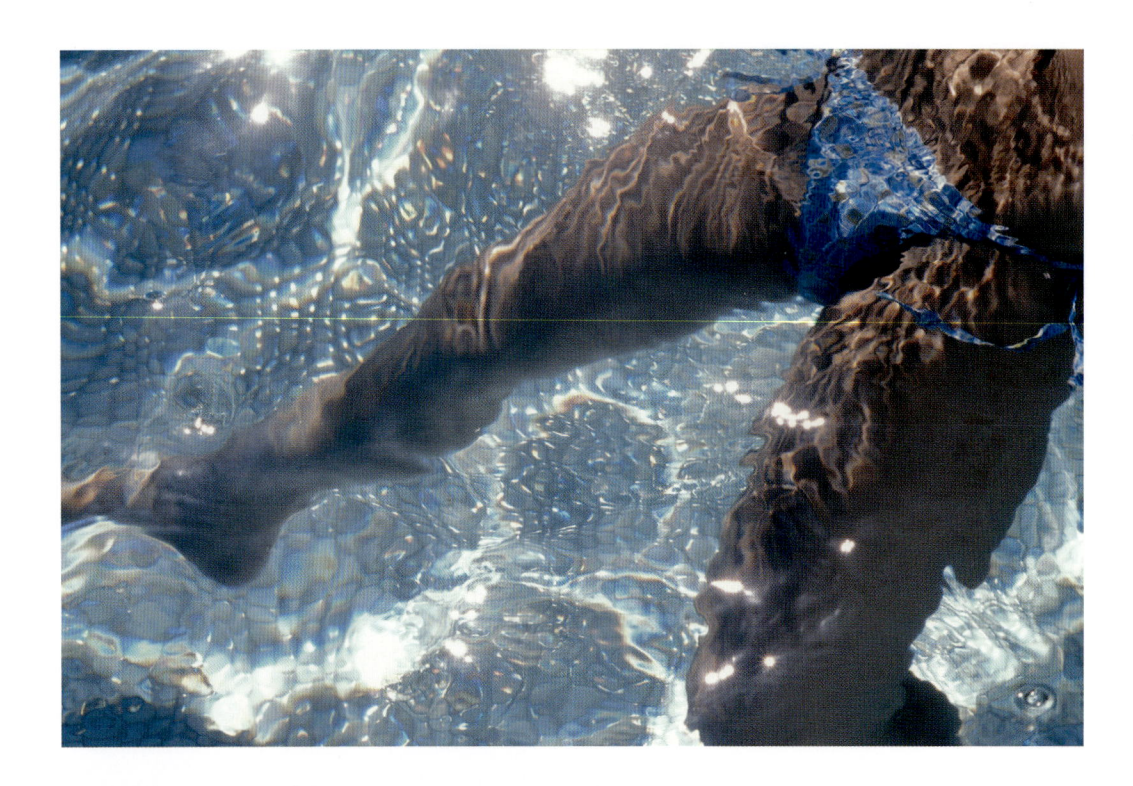

Then I become submerged completely. I am inside water. It penetrates all the pores of my skin. As I lift my arms and hands out of the water and put them back in, I feel the air on my wet skin, and then the silken smoothness of the water as my hand slides through it. Water-ness.

When I come upon an area or phenomenon bursting with many aspects of visual resonance, I find it most helpful to look at the whole realm, the whole area, and contemplate it: wait to be drawn in and then go in and look further where I am drawn.

This does not involve any strategizing or thinking about what would make the most interesting shot. As I survey the whole realm, I feel myself settle in, relax, and expand my awareness out further, until I am completely inside of the experience of being there. The world and its elements come out to meet me. The experience is very gentle, and very intimate. When I am magnetized by something, I am pulled in. As I linger, I appreciate, and I resonate. If I feel a sense of commitment, of unconditional connection, my mind begins to shift towards how to express my perception accurately. When I finally push down the shutter button, I have made a complete relationship.

Within the place I am exploring, as individual flashes occur I take my time and shoot each one as if it's the only one. These are discreet perceptions, each one its own special expression. If I let myself become distracted by other possible perceptions while I am relating with one I have chosen, my circuits get fried and I find myself overwhelmed and dissatisfied by the shallowness of my experience.

I become ill at ease and worried that I "cannot get it all." This is like a person looking at a feast and feeling a sense of anxiety because it is not possible to eat the whole thing in one bite. In order to be fully satisfied by our visual feast, we have to thoroughly process and savor it.

Even the most experienced photographer can get carried away with excitement when coming upon a realm of visual wonder, especially if this realm is moving and changing while being observed. It can take us over. This is a major obstacle to being fully present in the midst of what is unfolding around us.

We become the hungry hunter who will not be denied. We lose our seat of being still and unmoving, and our ability to enjoy the experience and relax with it is compromised.

During one of our courses in Boise, Idaho, we took a field trip to the pedestrian mall. A large group of Korean ladies in traditional dress appeared and we couldn't believe our good fortune. We had discovered the mother lode of color, texture, and beauty. At some point I realized I was frustrated that I couldn't get inside the experience. I felt I was just an observer, a child begging for candy. This was a very challenging revelation.

With all of it right in front of me to experience, the biggest obstacle to receiving it was my sense of wanting to get it all, at once. I began to talk with some of the ladies, to move gently around them, smiling and connecting. I lost my sense of self-consciousness and was able to move inside of the moment, becoming a participant rather than an observer.

This type of shifting situation is something I work with over and over and it's one of the greatest tests of the stability of my mental stillness.

As Michael Wood has said, "It's a test of our mettle, how well we can hold our seat in a chaotic situation." All I can do is stay as present and loose as possible. If the realm of perception involves a group of people, I tune into the movement and feeling tone of the event, watching how people seem to feel about being there and with each other. I blend in with that. It's like being on a boat as it rocks and heaves in rough water. First I find my balance, my ground, and feel my place in the midst of the movement. Then I turn my awareness out and feel my physical being in the environment so I don't become ungrounded and panic. I become aware of my breath, and I feel my awareness go out gently. I survey the whole, and then begin to move to where I am drawn. This is how it works. I am not a hunter looking for a trophy, I am part of the fabric of this moment, and, in this present moment, my life is unfolding right now, right here.

18   Sad Joy

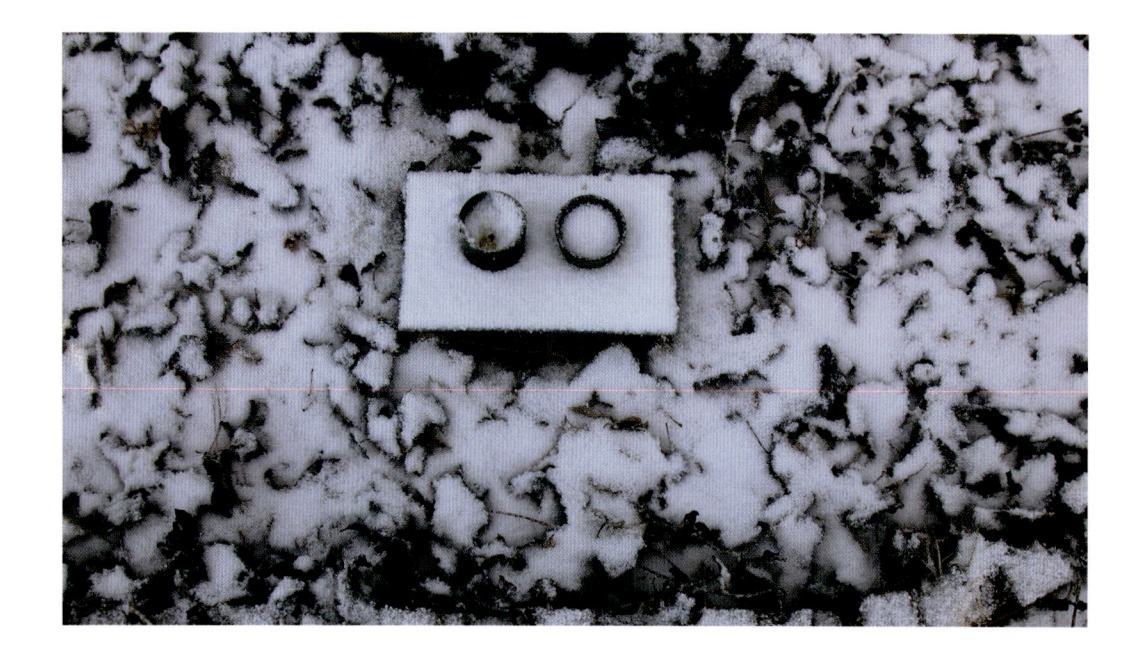

Loneliness

The sense of openness and vast possibility that happens as our solid sense of "this" begins to fall apart can make us feel intimidated, even very much alone, as we go out to explore our visual world. We miss our formulas, our certainty. It seems our strategies for managing our relationships do not bring us the intimacy of connection we long for. Feeling lonely while we are shooting is a good sign. It means we have given up all hope of being saved by something outside of our experience of the present moment. We begin to experience a shift in our allegiance from conceptual mind to direct experience. It is a very intimate and personal journey. Once we have tasted direct experience—we want more.

We feel so tender, so exquisitely soft, as if our heart could break. We don't know what to do or think. We just have no idea. A fly buzzes around our glass of water. We would like to make sure it does not get inside the glass.

And yet the feeling of the buzzing sound in our body and mind resonates so deeply that we do not move.

"Don't move.
Just die, over and over.
Don't anticipate.
Nothing can save you now, because you only have this moment.
Not even enlightenment will help you now, because there are no other moments.
With no future, be true to yourself, and express yourself fully.
Don't move."

Shunryu Suzuki Roshi

Seeing as Receiving

The hallmark of direct seeing is that we receive. We cannot receive until we surrender our agenda, our spin, because until then, there is no willingness to accept. We do not believe that we will receive, and we are afraid we will fall flat and look and feel foolish. Maybe we can't abandon our strategy of seeing without knowing we will get something in return worth getting. In direct seeing, there is no measuring. And there is no one who cares about keeping track anymore. It is like being lost in the middle of the ocean and realizing no one knows you are lost. You may have to give up hope of ever being found. You may have to surrender your hope of returning to shore.

When we finally do give up, we begin to notice that a subtle shift has occurred.

Our mind has become very still, our body stops moving, and our eye stops hunting. Our sense perceptions have expanded so that sounds are penetrating, sights are vivid. Then our visual world comes up to meet us. It is here, in the receiving, that we make contact.

Letting go strengthens our sense of stillness and stability. We let go, we open, and then we receive. This is how the whole thing works. It is the ground, the path, and the fruition of this practice. This is what we are always developing throughout our journey of direct seeing.

Making contact with our visual world is not anything we can manufacture or strategize. It is similar to being in a culture so different from ours that we have no points of familiarity or reference. We have no idea what anyone is saying to us. The sense of connection to our place, to our identity is absent. In fact, you could say we experience a signal drop out. Our homing beacon has disappeared. We are not on radar. We are naked and vulnerable. This is not a bad thing. We are free, our mind is free, and we are floating with our eye, our mind, and our heart to direct us. We can accommodate anything, effortlessly. The more we let go of all our ideas, the more room there is for us to be touched. Because there is no push or pull, we can actually meet our world.

The Smile of Recognition

My friend has a new granddaughter. Her first six weeks of life have been an adjustment to her body and her new world, and she hasn't appeared to be able to focus and recognize particulars in her environment. She has been working on it, but the chaotic home with other young children is a lot to take in. The first monumental task of a baby is to align the sense perceptions with the mind that can distinguish this from that, understand familiarity and context, and integrate that with the ability to put all together in one moment of recognition. This is a very deep and profound process; it establishes orientation and connections that will endure a lifetime.

His daughter Sarah called to report on baby Scarlett, and to tell him about a moment that will no doubt always stay in Sarah's memory. Sarah and her family had succumbed to strep and the flu. Sarah was exhausted. Her other children were crying and miserable. In the midst of this, late one night when the baby was feeding and Sarah was wondering how she could stay awake, she suddenly noticed that Scarlett's face had transformed into a big smile from ear to ear. She was fully present and looking at her mother. It was a moment when Scarlett's eye, mind, and heart clicked into place. It was Scarlett's first smile of recognition.

In our discipline of direct seeing, we work to return to this basic state of perception so we can experience and connect with our world with simplicity and directness. We experience Scarlett's smile of recognition every time we dissolve into a sense of appreciation and connection with our perceptions. Just like baby Scarlett, we feel the joy of deep, unconditional relationship.

The Tender Open Heart

Why are we willing to let go, to be so bold, and to explore beyond our zone of comfort? It is because we have found our strategies failed us. At some point along the way, as we were trying to do what we felt was being asked of us, we realized the truth. Struggle is not going to solve the fundamental issue of not fully participating in our world. It is just not going to do it. At some point it becomes obvious to us. We just let go. And as we do, an opening occurs. In this moment real perception and real meeting take place.

This is where we experience a sense of poignancy about our lives, that we try so hard, we all try so hard, we all try so hard to be good, and we all try so hard not to experience more suffering. We always try to make ourselves feel better.

At some point—maybe at the moment we die, or at the moment we realize that all of our strategies are really not accomplishing what we want them to fundamentally—we give up. We surrender, and we let go. And when we do, there is something else there.

There is tenderness, an open-heart quality. Just a sense of, "I'm here. I'm just here. I'm here. Someone, some thing, will you play with me? Will you come be with my tender heart? Will you love me?" That is the longing, the basic longing that we all experience, and that has all come about because we actually let go. Letting go is a primal situation. It is where we cross the border between what we want, how we've lived, and who we are, into another unknown and undefined region where anything is possible and we don't know. And this is where our actual wisdom starts to shine. It shines through and reaffirms our fundamental sense of well-being. It is good to be a human, here on this earth, right now in this moment. That's how it happens, over and over.

Resonance

When we feel our heart touched by something we see, it is not because we are sad or melancholy. It is a physical experience of expansion and connection. Something deep within us is stirred. This is resonance. It can happen even when we notice the smallest detail.

For example, this morning I made myself a bowl of cereal. It was puffed grains of all kinds, and the surface was a combination of very light shades of beige. As I poured the white stream of milk over the puffed grains, I noticed there was a tiny piece of green parsley among the puffs, just one tiny piece, all on its own. I could have said, "Uh oh! There is a problem in my cereal. How did that parsley get in there?" But it was so delicate, so tentative, green totally surrounded by beige, with little rough edges. It was sticking up ever so slightly from the surface so it could be seen. As I continued pouring the milk, the tiny sprig disappeared, becoming submerged beneath the puffs. I felt the whole thing in my body and mind together. My heart swelled. I was not sad; I was touched in my tender heart, somewhere in my being where it feels good to be touched.

EFFORTLESS BEAUTY

SAD JOY 148

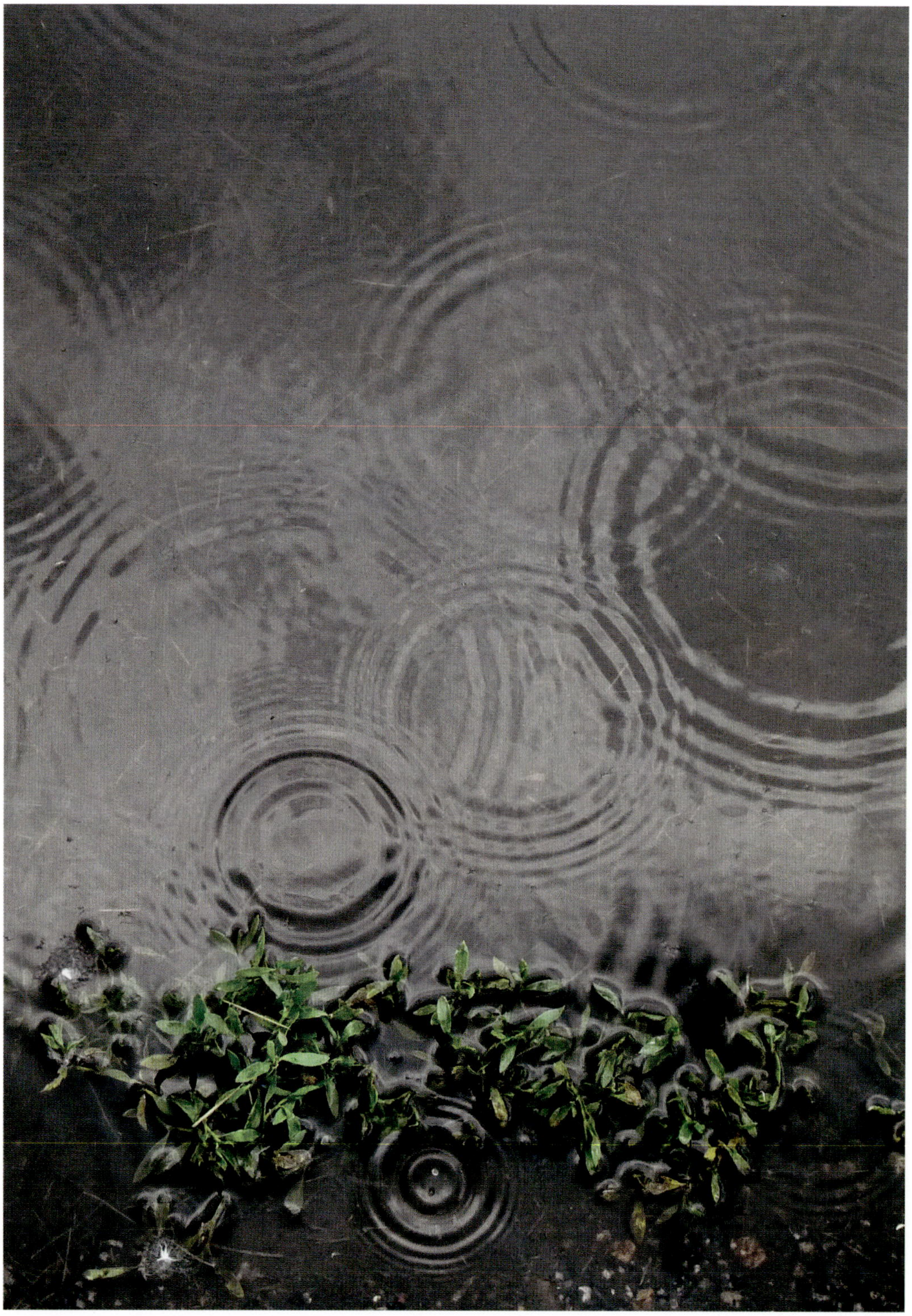

SAD JOY 150

EFFORTLESS BEAUTY

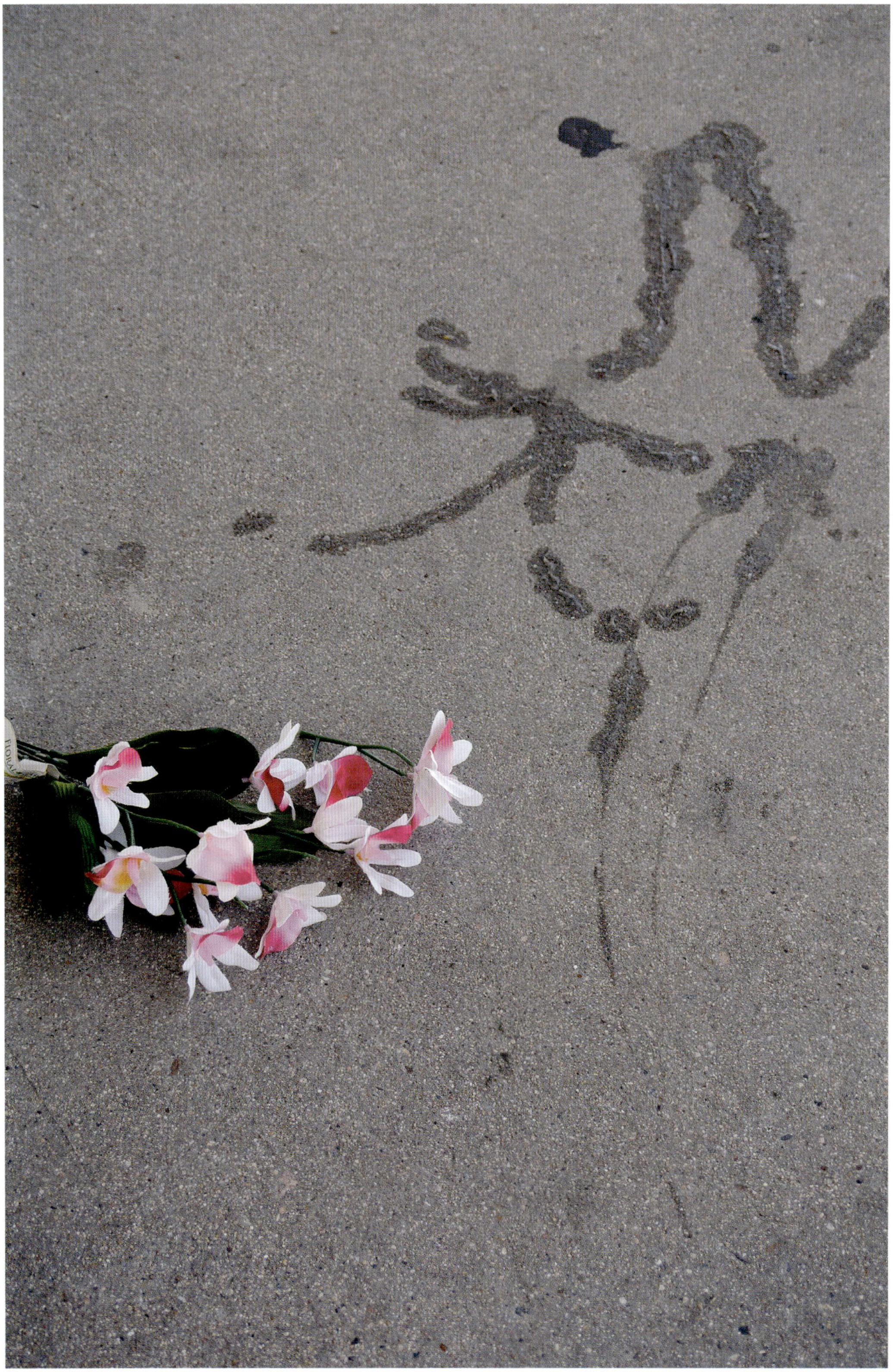

19   The Heat of Direct Perception

The Door is Open

When I feel like going out with my camera, I am going out because I want to see. I want to connect with the fire, the heat that is direct perception. I take myself as I am, whether I am sick, depressed, restless, or happy, and I throw myself upon the world, asking to be met. As the Buddhist nun and teacher Pema Chödrön has said, "You start where you are." I am willing to relax and suspend my point of view without asking for anything in return. I am feeling generous, expansive, open, and ready to play.

It is with this state of mind that I begin to walk around and look. I pay attention to the sensation of my body as it moves across the pavement. I breathe, I look, I feel the air as I move through it and it blows against my skin, the warmth of the sun, the moisture in the air. I don't know anything except that I am right here, right now. As thoughts come up in my mind, I bring myself back to the simplicity of my feet on the pavement. With each footstep I dissolve my thoughts and come back to right now. My thoughts don't interest me nearly as much as the possibility of discovery. As my thoughts become less frequent, I begin to settle into my body. My mind is alert, awake, and my intention is to see. My eye and mind seem united in the purpose I have set for myself.

For this time, I am like an alien in this world; everything else exists, and always has, just as it is. I am a lone person on the planet to whom nothing is familiar. I depend upon a moment of grace to communicate, to make a connection. Out of the blue, I am met. My mind becomes still and silent. All sounds recede, time stops.

I feel I'm in a new realm of experience. I look at what has presented itself, and my curiosity propels my investigation into its nature.

What is it? What has caught my attention? As I look at it and feel its qualities, I understand its expression fully in my mind and my body. I am absorbed in the experience as I open to it and it fills my senses. I am no longer aware of my separateness. My senses are heightened and everything is vivid and brilliant. I feel alive.

Falling in Love

When I engage in the discipline of direct seeing I deliberately enter a realm of possibility. I am so curious about the world and so eager to connect with it that I often feel that I am opening myself to new relationships. And over the years that I have done this practice, my relationships have evolved with it so that both in my personal relationships and my visual relationships, I don't settle for insincerity or small talk.

For me to engage with someone or something, the relationship has to be based upon openness. From that ground arises respect and appreciation of the goodness that is there, that is expressing itself. There is an initial moment of engagement; something is percolating under the surface. Something comes forth to meet me and I am intrigued. I want to know more, investigate further.

This is not a casual flirtation. I have been met and I have connected. I trust that this is the genuine deal because I don't know what else it could be. I couldn't make this up—it's too outside my zone of familiarity. It comes out of nowhere. I can't control it. If I can hang in there and stay with the moment without trying to be cool or smart, if I can stay totally open and without artifice, then there's a chance that I can connect fully.

When I am open, something actually comes out to meet me. Great surprise, the world comes out to meet me! When that happens, all struggle seems to fall away and I experience my object of interest vividly, fully. I begin to melt. My heart feels so tender, so alive, like a vibration of space within me. Suddenly I know that I must commit to this experience, this perception.

There is no deliberation, no hesitation. I raise my camera, adjust my depth of field and exposure, determine that what I see through the viewfinder is nothing more or less than the perception. I seal the experience when I push the button.

I lower my camera as the experience begins to dissolve and rest in the sense of dissipation. Letting go, open space. Then, I walk away. I have been deeply touched.

THE HEAT OF DIRECT PERCEPTION   156

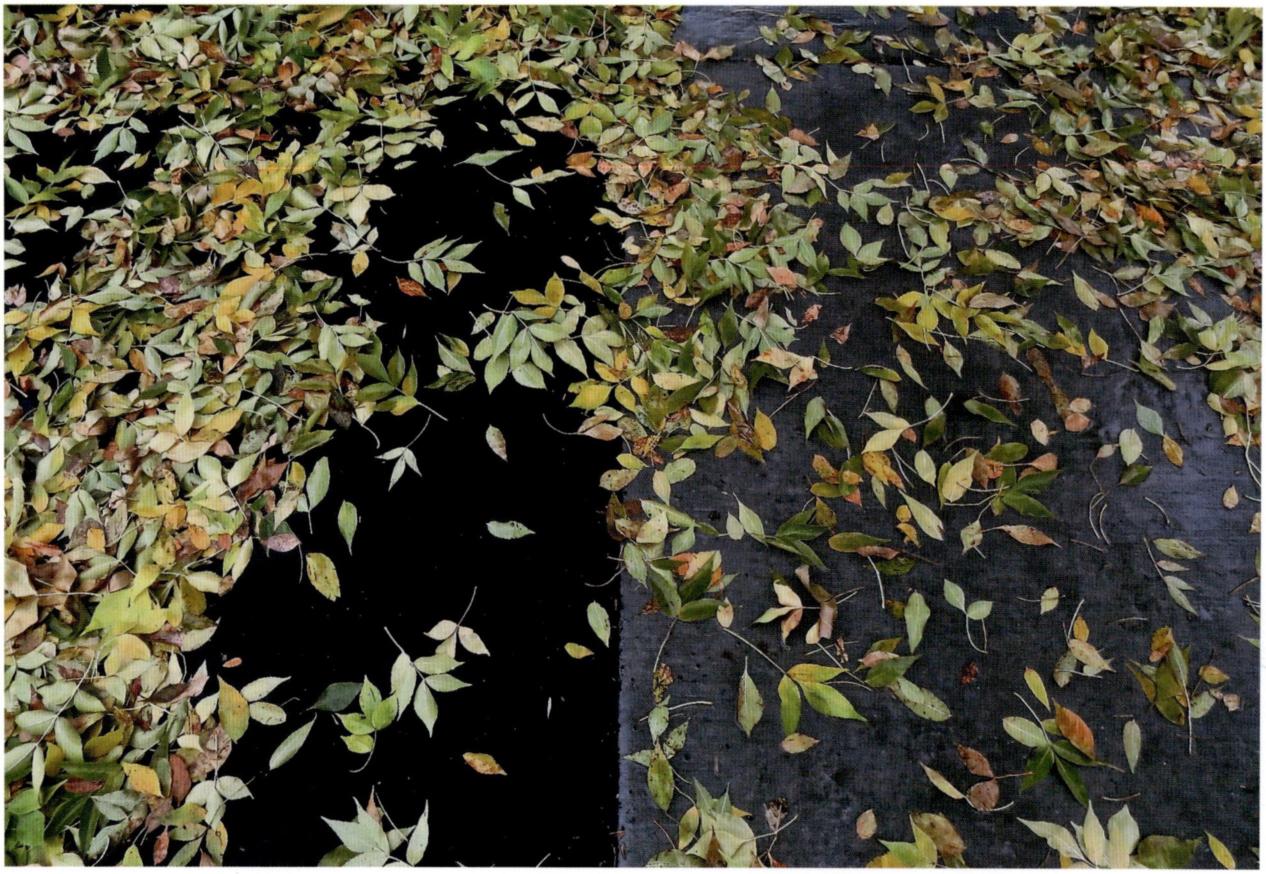

THE HEAT OF DIRECT PERCEPTION   158

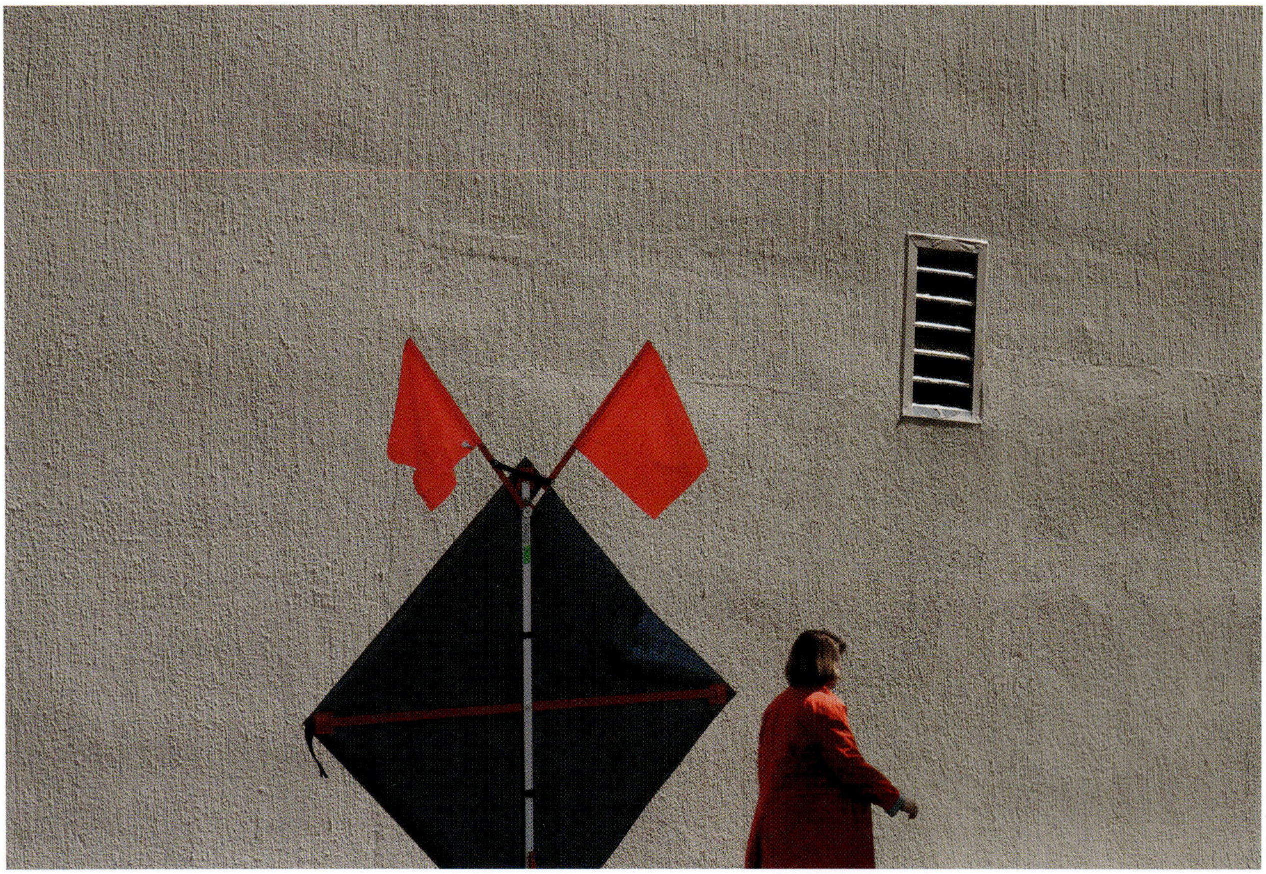

THE HEAT OF DIRECT PERCEPTION 160

20 Visually Conscious Living: Making Room for Beauty in our Lives

Paying Attention

In order for us to be able to experience and photograph a fresh perception, many factors must be present in that moment. We have to have stillness of mind and an intention to be available to see. Then we have to be physically present where what we see is. The light has to be illuminating what we see in a particular way so that we can see it. The components of the perception, the color, the light, the movement, the gesture, the coming together of disparate elements just so, have to be present long enough for us to see them, and then we need just long enough to form the equivalent of our perception with our camera. This is a very special set of circumstances. It occurs only once. And because we are paying attention and not self-absorbed, because we notice our world, a splendid display can manifest for us any time. And to express this experience, we have to have our camera.

My camera is not big or heavy. I don't need to feel that I am a "professional photographer" or a "serious photographer". For me it's about the joy of seeing, and feeling able to do that anywhere. A small camera with good parts is perfect for carrying around with me wherever I go. For instance, when I get out of the car to go into the grocery store, I can easily reach down and pick it up to bring with me. It's amazing to me that each time I talk myself out of bringing it along, I have a unique, vivid perception that I long to photograph.

Lately I have been working most of my waking hours. My mind has become overloaded with the tasks I perform, the minutiae of detail that pass through my mind. When I feel so overwhelmed, I find that what I have learned from this practice has given me great benefit. I have the steadiness of a trained mind and eye. No matter what is going on in my life at work or with my family, my "Good Eye" is always available to connect and to appreciate. I feel very grateful to my wonderful teacher, Michael Wood, for this. And because I carry my camera with me everywhere I go, I am reminded to be available to the perceptions I can have no matter what I am doing or where I am.

I am not looking every moment of the day. I don't actively scan the environment all the time to see if there is anything that magnetizes me. Mostly I'm solving puzzles, problem solving. I don't like doing two things at once, as neither one gets done well. But on another level, a deeper one, I am available to be stopped by a perception. I'm always paying attention. I could be stopped by a perception anytime, anywhere.

I could suddenly notice a pen on my desk as the light hits it and illuminates its blueness. When my daughter stops by my office, inevitably I become magnetized by the color of her tank top, the line of her neck, the color of her skin in the light. My colleagues know that when they come to talk with me, they may be photographed. When we have snow or rainy weather, I open my office window and pay attention to what is going on outside. I may be feeling overwhelmed by what is happening in my life, but my awareness is directed outwards. My antenna is calibrated towards openness to receive.

And when I do see, I connect. There is no separation between myself and what I see—no thought about it. For me it is pure delight. Suddenly I check in fully to the here and now. The preoccupations of my busy mind have been cut through by a diamond knife, and my awareness is fully present. Time stops; the totality of my concentration on my work pauses. My mind is still. I stop what I am doing.

I take time to look fully at what I have seen. I take time to drink my fill. How does it feel? What is its quality? What elements are present? I take time to appreciate all of its aspects, and my heart is touched by this moment of intimacy. It has come to me out of the blue. How could this happen? It feels like magic. It is a moment of graceful appearance.

Being Deliberate is a Lifestyle Choice

The natural evolution of having a mind of simplicity is that we direct our attention to one thing at a time. This gives us the psychological room, the spaciousness of mind, to take our time and fully notice the qualities of our world. We notice when our partner is pale and looks sad. We notice when the dirty clothes hamper is full. When we pick up our glass to drink we feel the contour, the textured surface of the glass. This is our world. It is good to live in it.

We work to develop our deliberate approach through our practice of being visually aware as we photograph. When we see directly, there is no random activity or sidetrack from our perception. We exert ourselves to pay attention from the beginning to the end, right through to the editing process. We are still, we are present, we are engaged, and within that, we are deliberate.

We plan adequate time to complete our project, properly and fully, whether it is a photography outing or the act of seeing itself. We don't want to rush any part of it. Before we begin to look, we establish clarity of intention. Then we see. We physically and mentally stop and look at what we have seen. When we fully understand its nature, we choose to seal the experience with an image. At this point we consider how to express what we are seeing, the technical aspects of the expression. Then we bring the camera to our eye. We check one last time through the viewfinder to see if our image is an exact expression of our perception. Then we seal the experience as we push down on the shutter.

Finally, we bring the camera down from our face, and rest once more in stillness with our perception before we turn away.

There is no arrogance, no idea that taking a short cut will get us where we want to go. Seeing directly involves looking, having intention, staying in the moment, being curious and passionate. There is nothing haphazard about it. We want to do it fully and be fully involved in what we are doing.

Because we practice in this way, over and over, the way we conduct ourselves has a potent effect on the way we choose to live our life. We always have a choice. Because we have disengaged the engine of impulse, of immediate reaction and judgment, and because we have learned to rest our minds in stillness, we are moving toward elegance. We thirst for elegance. We resonate with it. Elegance in this sense is the simplicity of things as they are, expressing themselves completely. Nothing is fabricated—it is completely genuine and true. Our lives become permeated with simplicity and well-being. We do not rise and fall with depression and excitement. We are steady, and from this comes a sense of confidence in the goodness of our mind and our world.

Ordinary World, Ordinary Magic

Perhaps the most wondrous of all aspects of direct seeing is the joy it brings us as we appreciate the everyday aspects of our life and our domestic world.

When we bring the mind of stillness and availability into our daily world, it is like a light bulb has been turned on. We feel we have never really looked at anything in our environment before. For example, my partner has gray hairs around his temple. He has lines going from his nose to his chin. His arms are long, and he floats as he walks. I realize I haven't really looked at my partner for a long time.

Our ordinary, personal world is so familiar that we don't look at any of it anymore. We already know how it looks. We worked that out a long time ago, so we don't have to do it again. And yet, as time has gone by, much has changed. Every day it has changed, and continues to change. The sun has shone through the window every day at 4pm for longer than I can remember, and it has illuminated the couch, the table, and the curtains in a very soft and inviting way. The sun beams into the kitchen every morning and no matter what is in the sink, it becomes a celebration of color, texture, line, and light. Each day is a new display, manifesting in a particular way for a short period of time. Then it changes. When we tune into this stream of circumstance, we discover ordinary magic.

It is helpful to park ourselves in different spots in our home or yard during the day, to settle into our still mind and begin to notice. At some point when we have thoroughly exhausted our thoughts about what we want to be doing and seeing, many little intimate details that we have never seen before will begin to emerge from the visual tapestry. This is the best of all things. It is our world, and yet it also exists as it is, on its own terms, in every moment. It is living, breathing, changing, adapting. We have a very intimate relationship already with our belongings, but we have not allowed ourselves to experience them visually, completely, in an ongoing way.

As my children were growing up, I worked at home. When I began practicing this discipline, I kept my camera close by me, whatever I was doing. It was here, in the stillness of my world, during the day when the children were at school, that I was able to bring the intention to notice my world together with the intimate aspects of my life. My dishes, books, papers, and bed all became magnets for perception. I could observe the daytime light working its way across the sky as it penetrated the interior light of each room, transforming everything in its path.

It is in this way that our home becomes our palace. Nothing is unnoticed, and we find we are arranging our things to suit our sense of visual balance and harmony. We may not have an idea of what this looks like in our minds, but it develops within us organically, like where we like to place our hairbrush or place our dishes in the cupboard. We know where it feels right to us. We know because we are paying attention to how the objects feel in the space and how we relate with them in that space.

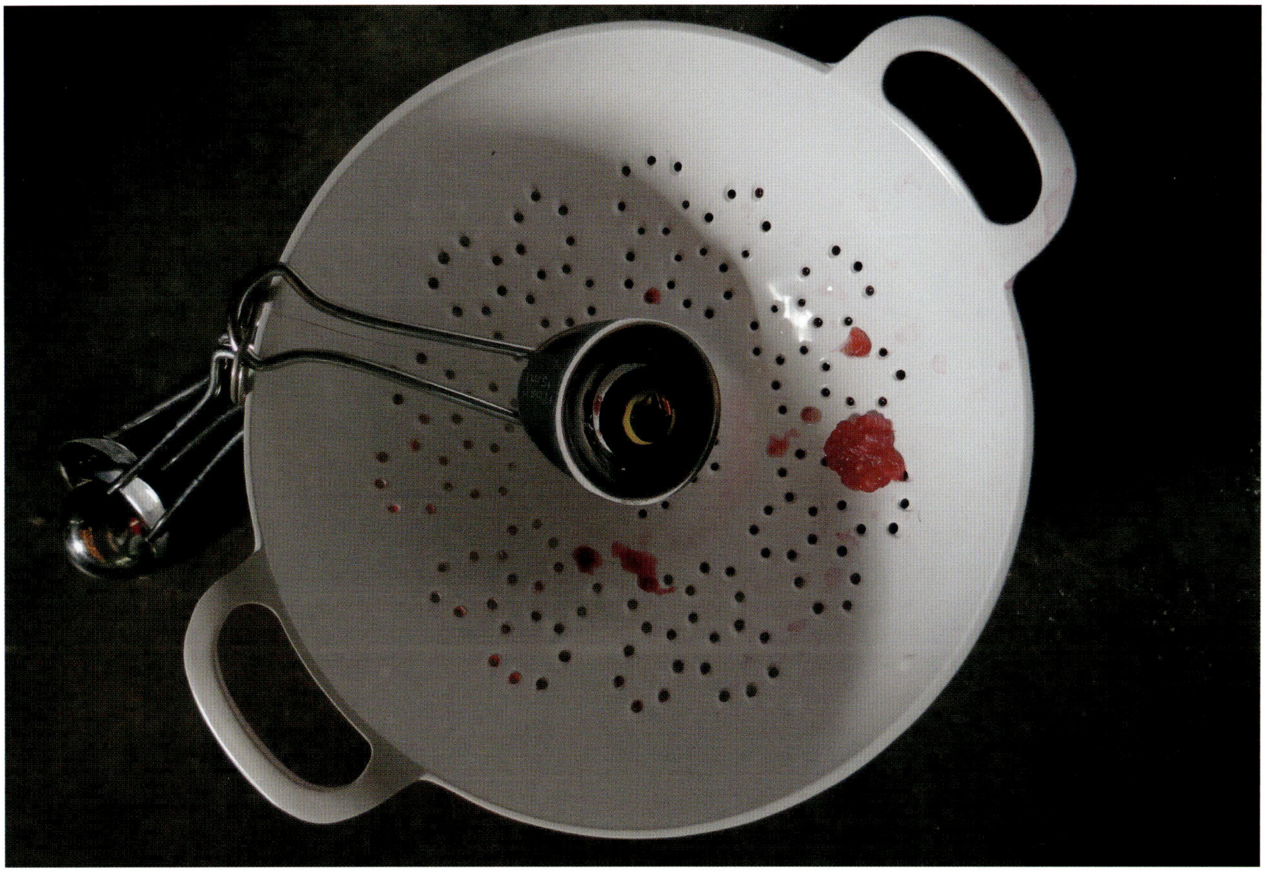

167 EFFORTLESS BEAUTY

VISUALLY CONSCIOUS LIVING: MAKING ROOM FOR BEAUTY IN OUR LIVES

EFFORTLESS BEAUTY

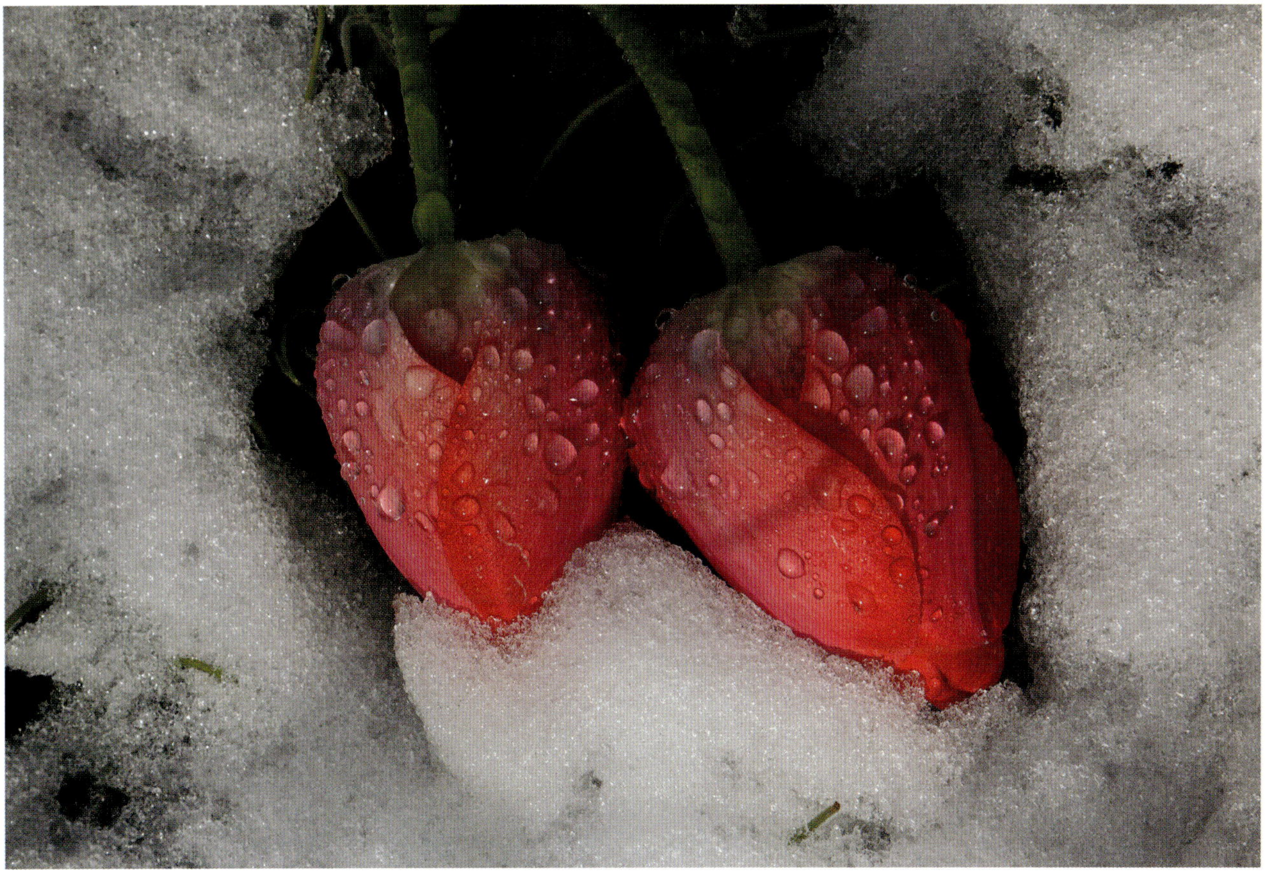

The Pond

A drop hits the water. A ripple begins and radiates from the middle, the point of contact, growing larger as it expands. The waves become thinner as the force of the outward expansion diminishes, until they subside and re-absorb into the water from which they came. Water dissolves into water as the surface returns to stillness. Water flows, it reflects, it changes form, but it is still water. Clear in nature, reflecting the world around it, the sky of blue or gray; whether the water is shallow or deep, the reflective quality is still there.

Our minds are like this when as newborns we experience our first perception, and in each moment of our lives sensation, perception, thoughts, and emotions create currents in the stillness of our mind. Sometimes they are like tidal waves or monsoons. Sometimes they are more like a light rain falling. Like waves in water, they are the expressive quality of our mind. Our experience is activated by a perception, which brings a ripple through our mind and body, until it subsides, and is reabsorbed into the mind from which it came. Maybe this is why we resonate so much with water. When we look into water that is still, it can feel like we are looking into a mirror. Just as still water can reflect back whatever is reflecting in it without any alteration, so our images can express what we have seen like a reflection in still water.

When I look into the water at our pond, I feel my mind become peaceful, even. The pond begins to reflect itself in my mind. Or is it that mind reflects in the water? Our nature, the water, and my mind are not different. Sometimes as I peer down into the pond, I feel like I am looking into myself. If it is still, I feel very still. Whatever it is, I melt into it.

VISUALLY CONSCIOUS LIVING: MAKING ROOM FOR BEAUTY IN OUR LIVES

173   EFFORTLESS BEAUTY

VISUALLY CONSCIOUS LIVING: MAKING ROOM FOR BEAUTY IN OUR LIVES   174

175   EFFORTLESS BEAUTY

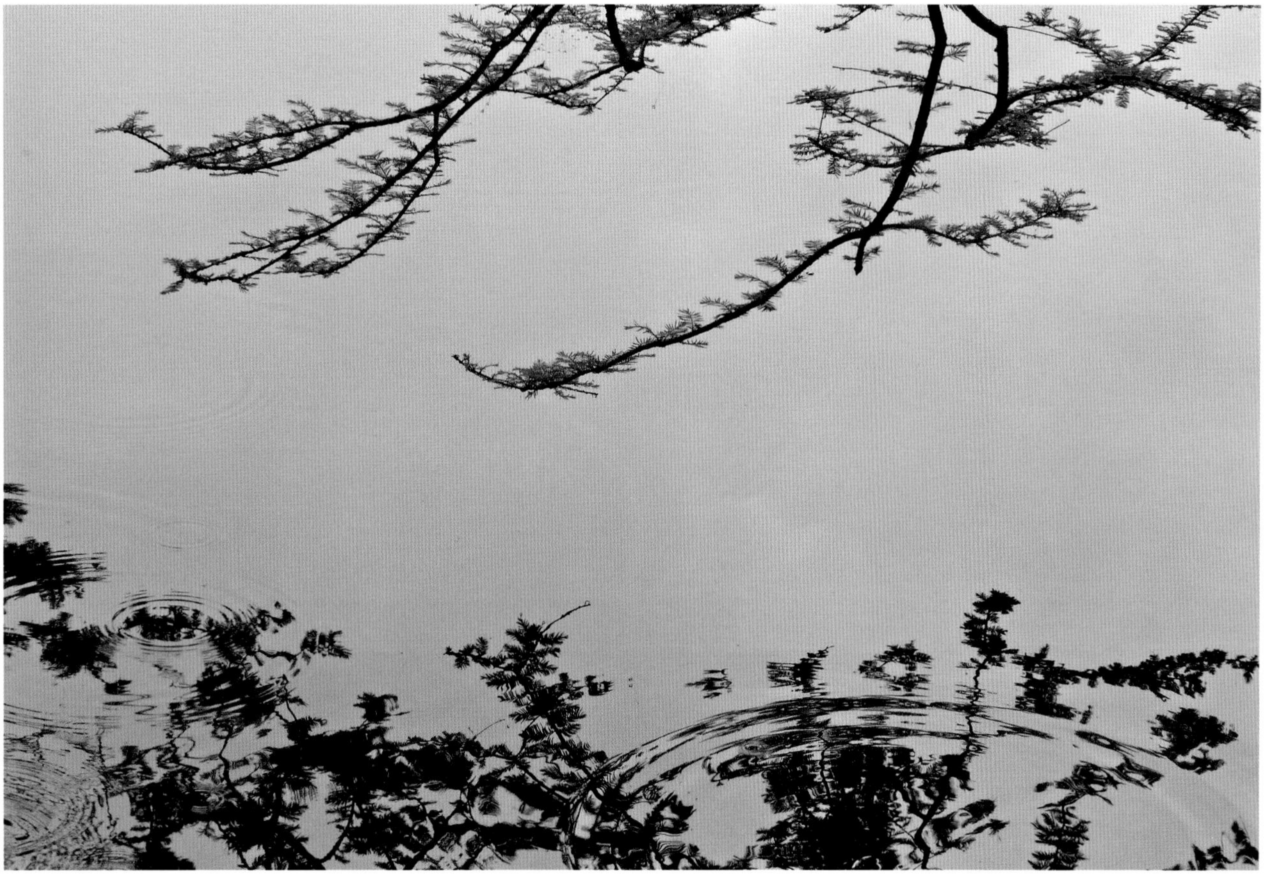

Our Home is a Palace

Every week, my partner Michael buys fresh flowers for our home. Why? I imagine it is because he appreciates his world so much. He beautifies it with flowers. He also brings home objects he has found that have qualities of elegance, simplicity, and presence. These seem to magnetize our visual awareness because they radiate their quality out into the environment of our home.

The flowers are often white, occasionally a pale color of pink. It touches me deeply that he connects to such an expression of intricate delicacy and impermanence. They are often photographed and fully noticed. As they fade, they are still appreciated.

This morning as I was in the bathroom, my eyes fell upon the floor mat draped along the side of the bathtub. A very pale gray line curved from the end of the mat around the contour of the while bathtub. It was so delicate, so rich, and so subdued that I resolved to get my camera.

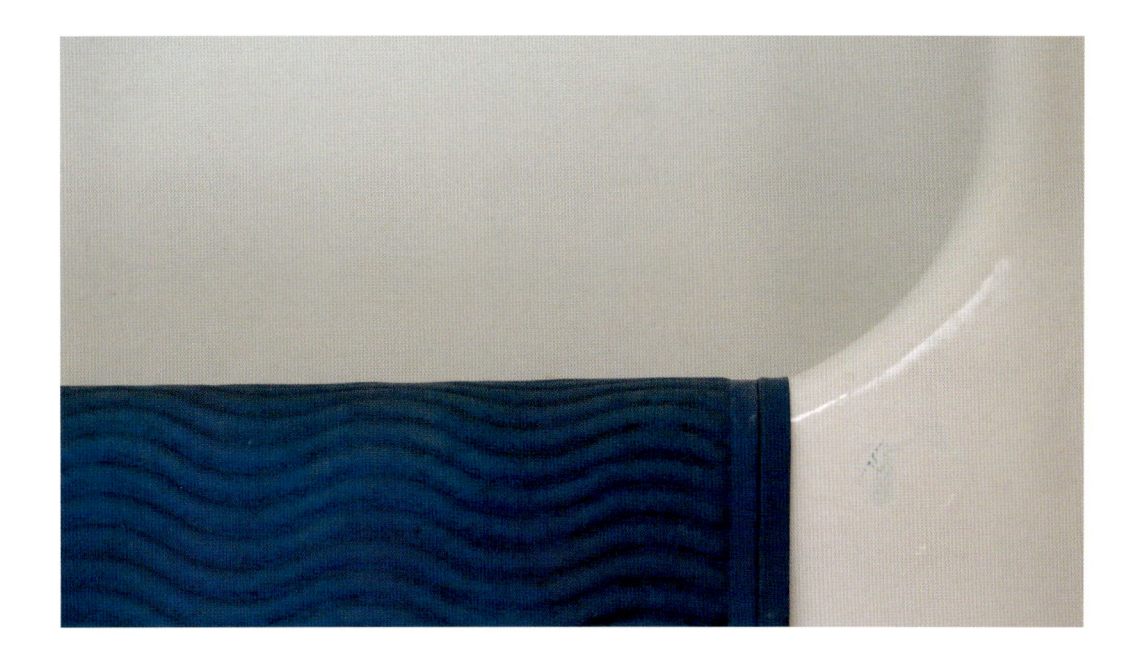

Upstairs, I realized that the sun was shining with illuminating vigor for the first time in five days. I remembered what Michael Wood had said many years before, "If I can't see in my backyard, where can I see?"

I went out the back door, down the steps. It seemed like everywhere I looked there were dry brown leaves covering the green grass.

In the garden there were damp leaves. Altogether it was a very rich situation. As I moved from one place to the next, I was delighted and moved by the arrangements of elements. When we feel our most personal environment intimately, when we allow it to penetrate us beneath our skin, down deep, the changes are so poignant.

There was one spot I didn't bother to look in my backyard this morning. I thought, There will be nothing there. Recognizing this attitude and how wrong it can be, I went over to take a look with a fresh perspective. I really could have missed out altogether on what was there, waiting to be noticed.

Then I wandered over to our patio table, the surface of which was strewn with leaves. It was such an elegant display.

Now I am having breakfast. I feel so happy, so enriched. With a world like this, how could I ever feel impoverished, needy? I am the queen of the palace of natural richness and splendor.

VISUALLY CONSCIOUS LIVING: MAKING ROOM FOR BEAUTY IN OUR LIVES

21 Essential Simplicity

Keeping It Fresh

Even as we remind ourselves to keep our perceptions fresh, we can come up against the realization that we see what we have already seen and photographed countless times. We can get tied up in knots, wondering whether we really truly see anything fresh. We have so many images stored in our memory banks that it can seem unlikely that we will be able to shoot anything that has not already been photographed. It helps to remember that we are not so concerned with the perception itself as we are with the freshness of our state of mind.

Authenticity in direct seeing is not so much about expressing a unique experience as it is about expressing our experience without drawing upon reference points to interpret it. These reference points are our labels, our point of view. This desire for originality is a good thing; we want to be certain that we are not emulating the expressions of others or drawing upon perceptual clichés. But ironically, this very desire for originality can involve the imposition of an external arbitrator whose job is to determine if our perception is an imitation or derivative from anything else. This desire can push us away from familiarity; and in another bit of irony, the familiar can be an important part of the discipline of direct seeing. The obstacle of familiarly doesn't mean that we don't want to shoot what is familiar to us, it means that we don't really look at our everyday world because we assume that it is not worth looking at because it is familiar.

Our habitual pattern is to believe that we have to go somewhere new and unfamiliar in order to have interesting perceptions. We can reject the familiar as subject matter because we think we are drawing upon a database of familiar subjects and images we have seen many times before. The problem is not that we are seeing things that have been photographed before, many times, but that we are not seeing those things through fresh eyes. The issue is never with what is being perceived, but with the state of mind that is perceiving. Our reference point is kicking in really fast, almost as quickly as the perception is arising in our mind, and that can be truly annoying. We are experiencing the obstacle of 'second thought' and then many more thoughts about the second thought. The result is frustration.

As with all art forms which concern themselves with authentic, direct experience, the process or path is the point. And once we think we have realized something about our process, we have a new guideline or reference point to measure our progress.

Fortunately for all of us, the end result of this struggle is to abandon struggle altogether. It is just too much mental work to figure out whether we're having a perception that is new to us. We would all like to get back to the basic enjoyment of our world. There is a simpler way in to this, an approach not based upon the Watcher within us judging what we do.

The Watcher splits us off from the moment and our experience, and is actually counterproductive. We have a saying, which we frequently use to help guide us through the conundrums that can come up in our practice—Feel Your Way. Go with how a perception makes you feel. Stick with the qualities of the fresh perception. I would memorize them. You can say to yourself, Am I shocked, disoriented? Did the perception come out of the blue? Is the experience buoyant and joyful? Just go back and forth between the words, what they mean, and then check in with how you are feeling. In time, when you recognize the familiarity of a perception, your appreciation of it will be there as well. And because you are confident and relaxed, you can let go on the spot of the Watcher, the back and forth, the self doubt, the second thought.

But if you are unable to simply let go of all of it, this could be an excellent time to turn away from the perception, close your eyes, turn back, and then look again in a fresh way. This is just like hitting the refresh button. At some point in your process you may decide to abandon the relationship, that you don't feel motivated to actually seal the experience. Or you may photograph it. In the end, what does it matter?

Are you fooling yourself? How do you know? When the experience is flat and you are working hard at it, not feeling confident, then you are not experiencing direct seeing, you are looking too hard. That is a sign that you are busy observing and editing your version of your experience. Whether or not we are having a fresh perception is not a problem that we have to solve with our conceptual minds. It's only a matter of being fully present.

Coming back fully to the present moment, clearing our minds, is the antidote for the conceptual knot of second thoughts. All of the thoughts about our experience of our perception are just our thoughts. Let them go. Dissolve the layer of judgment and the observer in your mind. Be patient, take your time, relax, and enjoy. The discipline of direct seeing is quite simple.

It is always simple. You do not have to be really smart to do it. You actually have to abandon your strategies of success.

Working with the Obstacle of Continuous Distraction

I would like to bring up an additional obstacle to this journey that is atmospheric, cultural, and pervasive. We have various degrees of involvement with it, and for some of us that is dependent upon the kind of work that we do. It amplifies and propagates the very influences that undermine our ability to have a still and peaceful mind, to be fully in the present moment for any duration. I am calling it the Obstacle of Continuous Distraction. This is not the same as the distraction of being inwardly absorbed. It is more about what happens to us as we engage with the world. It is helpful to acknowledge this obstacle and clarify our relationship with it, for without this clarity, Continuous Distraction will undermine any attempts we make to live a deeply satisfying life. This obstacle is called "continuous" because between the constant texts, phone calls, Twitter texts, Facebook comments, new products, emails, and the sense that we must keep up with everyone and everything all the time, we are continuously having to accept or reject attempts to capture our attention.

Because of the unrelenting quality of Continuous Distraction, it is a challenge to relax and settle our minds. We can often feel off-balance, overwhelmed, with a sense that something needs to be done or happen right away. This vague sense of dissatisfaction plays upon the restlessness of mind and amplifies it. With this itch-and-scratch approach, we relate to stimuli with only a fraction of our available attention, and we don't really relate to what anything actually is. Because we are distracted, we haphazardly label what we see and sometimes completely mistake what is really there. We don't experience fully, and we are never fully satisfied.

When you contrast this to a sense of peace, contentment, and joy, it is clear that this modern technological age can bring about enormous suffering arising from a basic sense of dissatisfaction. By participating in the consensual view that these distractions are a necessary part of living today, we can lose our sense of our own experience and what really matters to us in our lives. Continuous Distraction can become, by default, a lifestyle choice. Working with Continuous Distraction may be the greatest challenge of our age and what defines how we emerge from it as conscious human beings.

Conscious seeing is about being deliberate—deliberately being open and fully present. We have a constant choice in our lives generally as humans, and specifically as photographers. We can muddle through, constantly distracted and disengaged from our experience, or we can keep our eye and mind synchronized throughout our day. We can feel the texture of the moments of our lives. Bringing the practice of conscious seeing fully into our day-to-day experience is a potent and profound way to neutralize the perpetual distraction and restlessness that characterizes the modern techno-world in which we live. We do not have to talk on our cell phones as we walk down the street or as we stand in line to pick up our food. If we carry our camera with us, it can remind us to notice our world. We can always choose to experience our experience instead of being continually distracted.

How the Practice of Conscious Seeing Disrupts Continuous Distraction

The ground from which direct perception arises is our open, undistracted mind. Without having a mind that is available, we cannot make the electric connection of mind, eye, and the objects of perception. When we are reminded to notice our world, our training activates and we simply shift our attention to the present moment and its visual aspects. When we do this, our basic orientation catalyzes a sense of clarity about what we are doing. We become deliberate in how we approach the activity of looking, seeing, and photographing. As distractions occur, we stay on track and don't allow our thoughts and emotions to become the focus of our attention. Our cell phones may ring, but we don't have to answer! Once we notice this interruption has taken place, we can bring ourselves back once again to being open and available in the present moment (and hey, why not turn off our cell phones while we practice?). It's challenging enough to stay still and present without allowing Continuous Distraction to disrupt the stability of our discipline.

There is no doubt that if we integrate our practice of direct seeing fully into our lives that Continuous Distraction will lose its power over us. We will inevitably develop the possibility, and really the promise, that our continually distracted state of mind will be abruptly interrupted and penetrated by moments of sudden, shocking, vivid, brilliant, absorbing visual perception. We can stop and appreciate our world. It can be truly inspiring for us to be reminded that there is such a thing as living beyond Continuous Distraction.

Allowing Ourselves the Space to Be Undistracted

For those of us who meditate, many of us find that the time we carve out each day to connect with our basic being and unwind our mental preoccupations is the pause that refreshes. We create boundaries around our practice time; we decide we will not answer the phone or send or look at text messages. We know that if we don't consciously make decisions about what interruptions we will allow, we will end up sacrificing our practice time to the demands of others.

I encourage all of us to contemplate how we regard our practice. We can come to a workshop and go through the motions of doing the exercises and assignments.

But as long as we believe that conscious seeing is a hobby and not a practice, we will never allow ourselves the space for this ability to develop and deepen. If we are continuously distracted and interrupted as we work with this discipline, we cannot be still and experience our experience.

We can allow our conscious seeing practice the same boundaries and protection from external distraction that we allow for our meditation practice. If we honor our practice of seeing in this way, it becomes an integral part of how we experience our world, just as the boundary between our post-meditation experience and our meditation practice gradually becomes less apparent.

Keeping it Fresh/Working with Uncertainty

When I notice that I don't feel inspired to pick up my camera, I have to take an honest look at my state of mind. Sometimes work and family preoccupations seem to be relentless and I feel like I'm just a gerbil running on a wheel. In spite of that, the whole thing can be dissolved in an instant by the sharpest, most penetrating perceptions. There is no predicting it.

I have found that no matter what is happening with me, or how challenging my life is to my peace of mind, when I take my camera out to shoot I am surprised by how accessible my other mind is—the mind that is always there under the surface, behind my worries. It's always available, even though I may not be. When I establish my intention to be available, it's always there, waiting to shine through.

This mind is awake and without content of thoughts. It is not worn out by the circumstances of my life. I know that it is there because when I am paying attention, there are split seconds when I can experience it peaking out of the tiny crevices in the stream of my paying attention. I may think I'm paying attention, but when I notice that my mind is stopped for that split second, I have to slam on the brakes. I don't even know what has stopped me, but I have to check it out because it's outside of my usual way of looking. This is fresh.

For those of us who have been practicing direct perception for a while, and feel pretty good about the consistent freshness in our photographs, this feeling-good state is a slippery slope. We enjoy taking photographs because we love it. As I have lived and worked with this process of direct perception and made it a central part of my everyday life, I have accepted that the experience of direct perception is where the real joy is—not in the recycling of my previous flashes when I see something familiar and magnetizing. Feeling good is temporary, in any case, because it's bound to be followed by being not so sure about anything.

Since there is no formula we can use for freshness besides being open, available, genuine, and confident, each moment brings potential uncertainty. This is how I know I've got a chance of keeping my photography fresh. This uncertainty never goes away from moment to moment, because we aren't making it up. Our fresh perceptions come out of nowhere.

There is no relief in sight from the experience of uncertainty. Some try to banish uncertainty by joining a photo club and compromising their genuineness and confidence to the opinions of others. Fortunately, we don't have to do this. We can continue our process of seeing, of looking for what is truly fresh. We know it because we feel shocked, disoriented, fully awake, and joyful. We have the blood of explorers in our veins. We have thirst to go beyond the familiar. Uncertainty is a sign that we are awake and alive.

ESSENTIAL SIMPLICITY 188

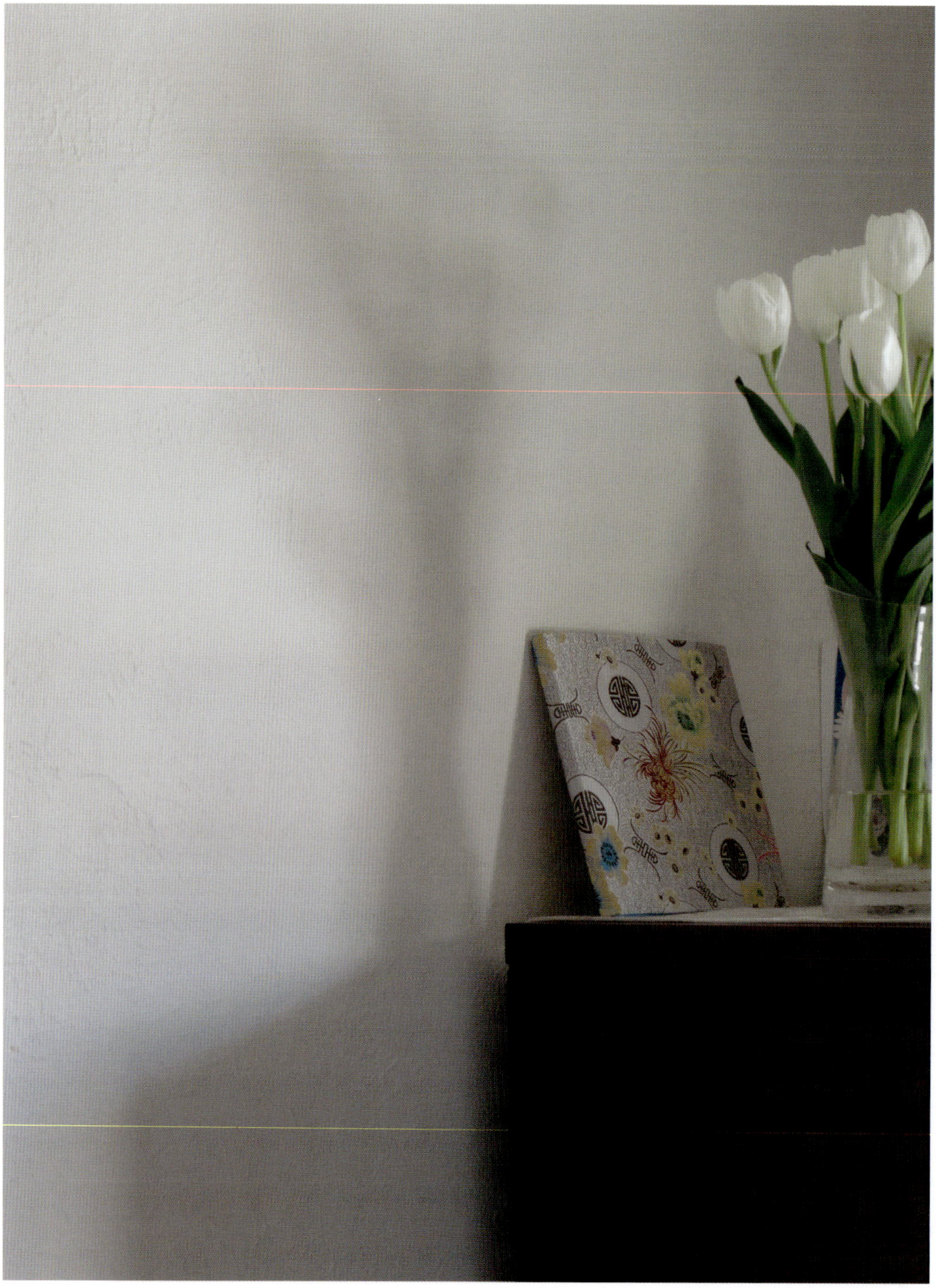

ESSENTIAL SIMPLICITY 190

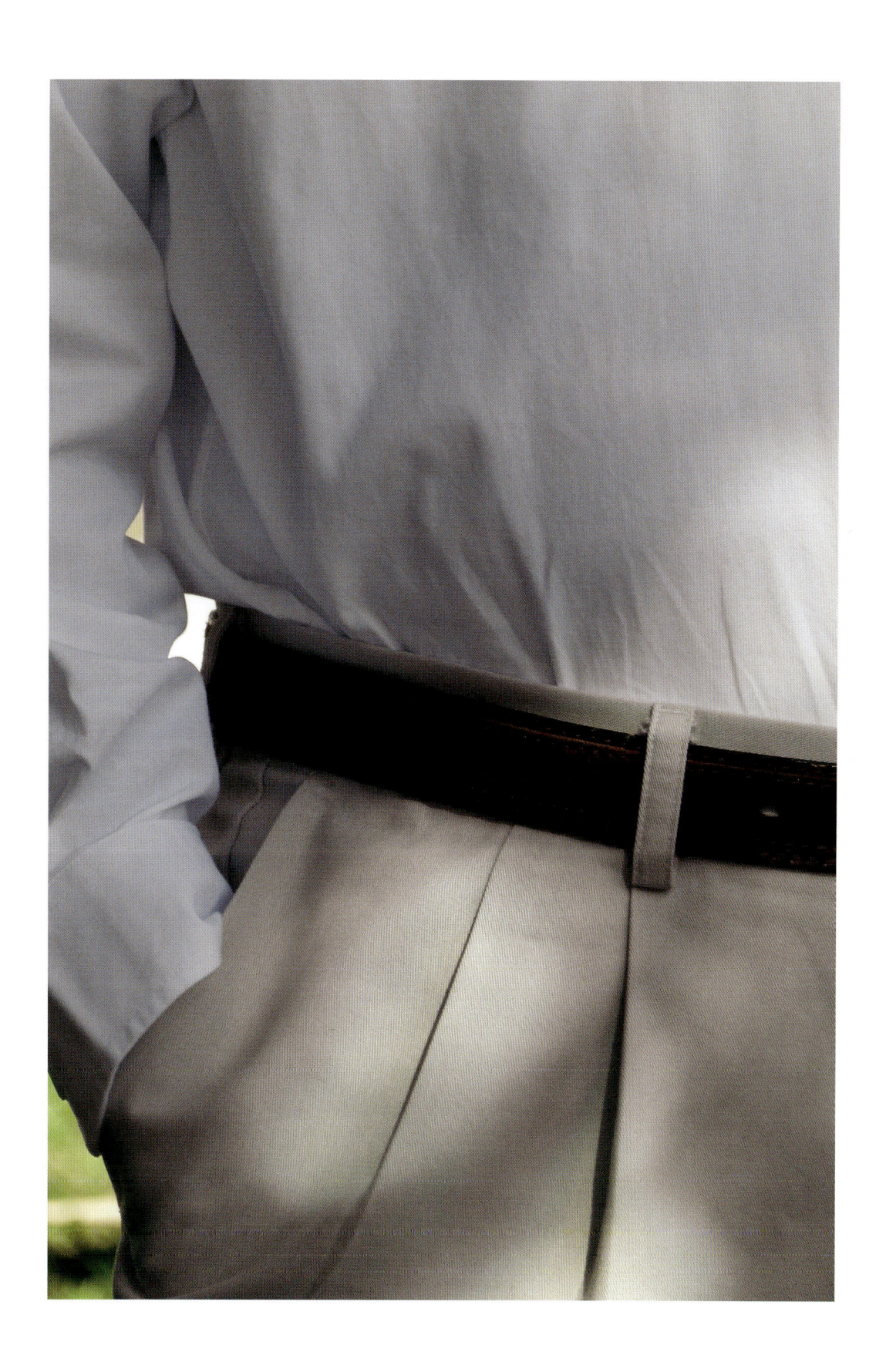

EFFORTLESS BEAUTY

ESSENTIAL SIMPLICITY 192

EFFORTLESS BEAUTY

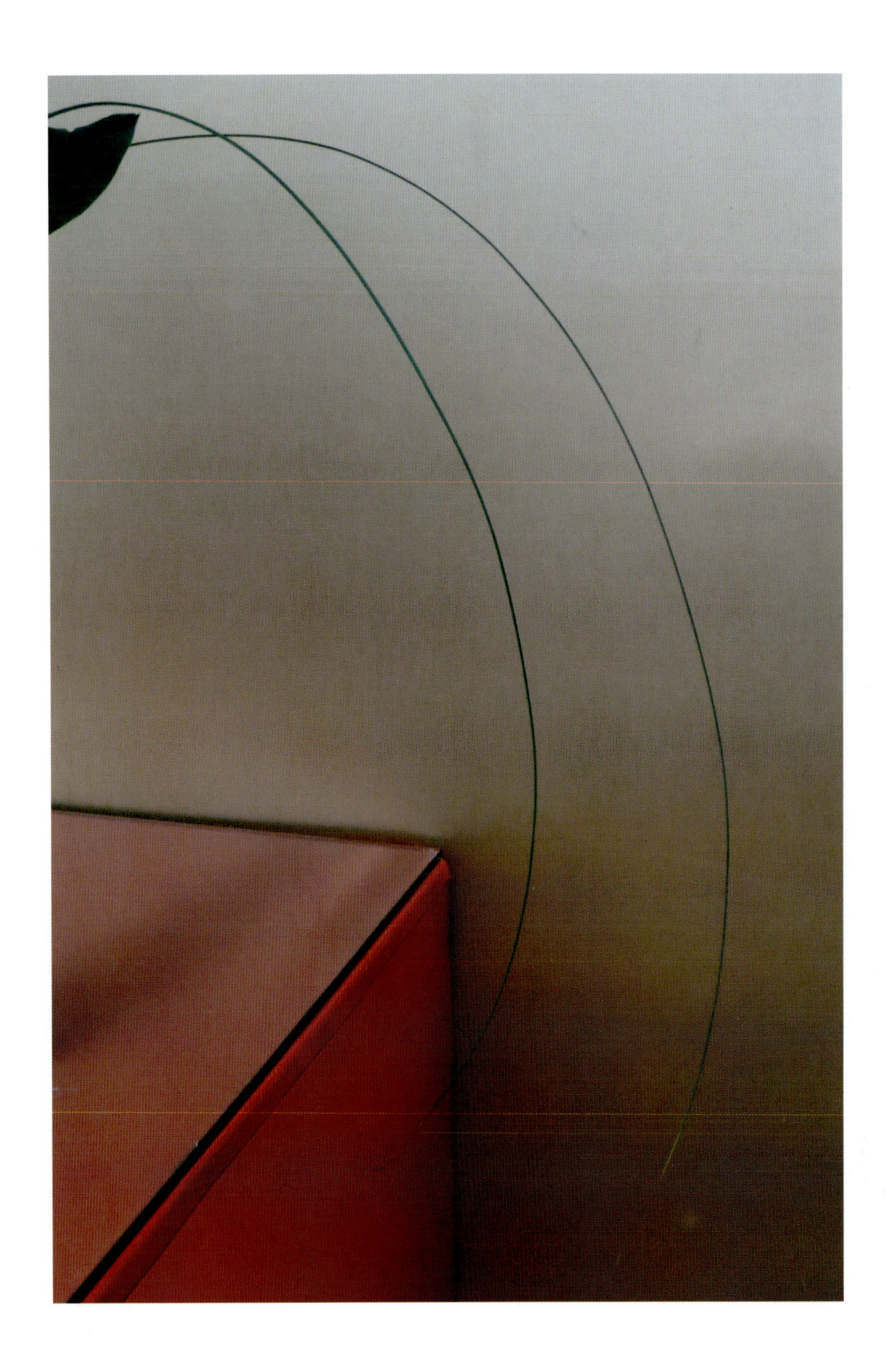

ESSENTIAL SIMPLICITY 194

22   Image Viewing as Practice

When we sit down at our computers to review our images, once again we settle our minds so that we can see our images with fresh eyes. If we fail to keep an open mind as the images come up on the screen, we may apply judgment and labels to them. We may not be able to reconnect with our original flash of perception or we may have doubt that we had one to begin with. We may ask ourselves if the perception is "interesting" and whether we could make it better. If we can't connect to the raw, direct quality of what originally stopped us, then we may have become disconnected from the thread of our experience.

But perhaps just as often, we just can't accept that the image we have taken is fine exactly as it is. If our mind was stopped by the perception, and the qualities of experience of direct perception were present, we fully stopped and took the time to thoroughly understand our perception, carefully adjusted our camera to express the quality of illumination, depth of field, and so on, with a mind of stillness, then the editing process is a confirmation of the experience. There is no need to improve upon what was perfect to begin with.

The uncertainty and doubt that comes up in the editing process are the same traps that presented themselves the very second that we had a perception. In the first moment that we experienced the perception, we had a choice: to stay with the freshness of what appeared to us, or to go with all of our thoughts and impulses about it. Now, in editing, we have that choice again.

The digital technology for photography is both a blessing and a temptation. Editing software is such that we can bring our image to express completely and accurately what we have seen. The adjustments we can make to our image allow us, if need be, to bring the colors into line with our perception and restore the balance of light and shadow to what we saw. We can eliminate, through cropping, any extraneous material in our image that was not included in our perception. With our original perception always in our mind's eye as our reference point, we can use this technology in a very helpful way.

On the other hand, often photographers will use post-production techniques to boost color saturation and add filters to the total image to achieve a desired effect. If we fall into this way of editing, our perception will be lost. We will have nothing authentic to share with our friends. When the image comes up on the screen, the freshness will be gone.

Editing is a Reflection of Our State of Mind

Editing is the final stage in the process of perception. It should not be like taking your perception to a plastic surgeon, to create something more glamorous. These perceptions are all fine just as they are; they stopped us and then we connected with them. We didn't connect with how they could be "improved." We just resonated, heart and mind, with how they were in that moment, falling in love. Then we committed to these perceptions and photographed them. When we fall in love, do we want to change it? Is it not good enough? Do we fall in love halfway, saving the rest for ourselves or for a better opportunity?

So it is with editing. Because we stopped, rested our mind, and appreciated fully what stopped us, we know our perception intimately. So the questions we ask while editing are entirely different from the usual approach. Now we ask, is it honest and full-bodied? Can we feel our mind in the expression of the perception? Is it as potent as it was in the moment when we were stopped? It's either a yes or a no. Yes means we were fully present and the image expresses the freshness of that moment. There is no halfway. If you don't know, or aren't sure what stopped you when you look at your image, you have no basis from which to edit. Eject. Delete, no second thoughts.

Here's the kicker. If there is no presence from the heat of direct seeing in the image, we have to hit the delete button. If the image feels lukewarm, compromised by uncertainty, it is not truly direct. We are not struggling to become acceptable photographers, admired by the experts. We don't wallow in our self-doubts. Eject. Let go. There is no point to our struggle. It is either a result of direct seeing, or it isn't.

We want to be genuine and authentic, not expressing second-hand perceptions. If the image doesn't communicate the perception, it's not going to have any juice. If it doesn't have the juice of direct, raw experience, then who cares? This is my attitude.

I'm not going to entertain and accommodate any uncertainty in my image gallery. I want my images to be free of all projections and manipulation, full and complete expressions of my experience.

Editing in this way is a learning process that takes time and effort. What if we're not sure if the image is a yes or a no? Maybe we're not sure if the perception really stopped us or if it was an idea of something we thought would work when we showed it to our friends. Maybe the perception is something we saw someone else shoot and everybody liked it.

These can be subtle aspects of our familiar database of images. We really watch out for this because if we go down this road of safe, comfortable familiarity, we risk losing our genuineness and our joy. If we really look with an open mind and look again, we will know if it is fresh or familiar. Eventually we lose interest in the familiar and save our fresh images. This is editing free of struggle. Quick, simple, samurai-style.

Editing is a reflection of our state of mind. Are we decisive and clear? Are we confused and lacking confidence? Do we look to others to tell us if our images are good or not? Are we fearful about making a mistake? If we make a wrong choice will we be criticized? Can we be daring and brave to show our perceptions, even if we don't know where they came from or why we shot them? Can we let go of the images that didn't work, and hit the delete button without agonizing?

For us, editing requires the three confidences: clarity, genuineness, and decisiveness. Our ability to fully manifest these qualities in our editing determines whether our images will be full expressions of our original perception. They are the measure of the accomplished practitioner.

EFFORTLESS BEAUTY

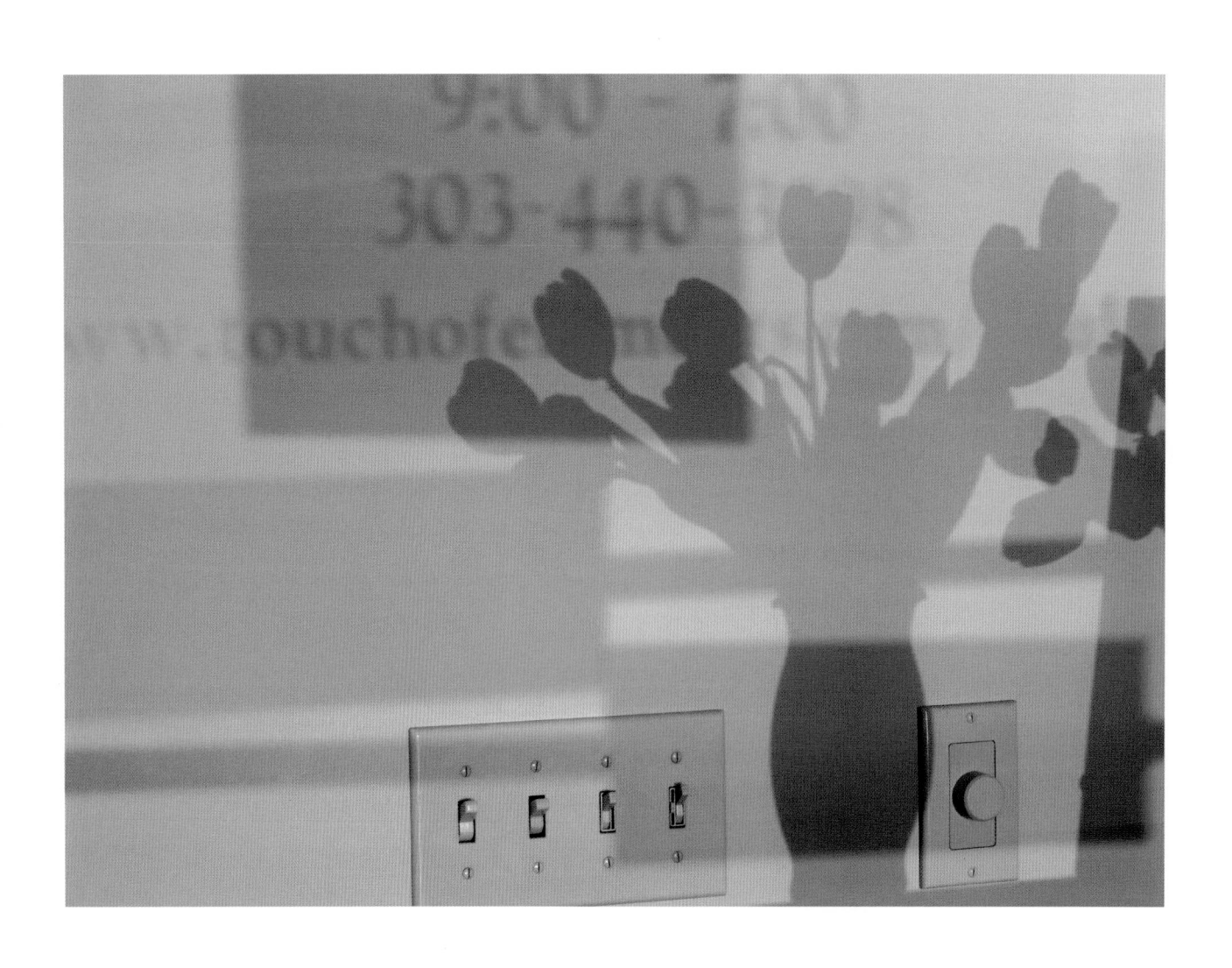

IMAGE VIEWING AS A PRACTICE   200

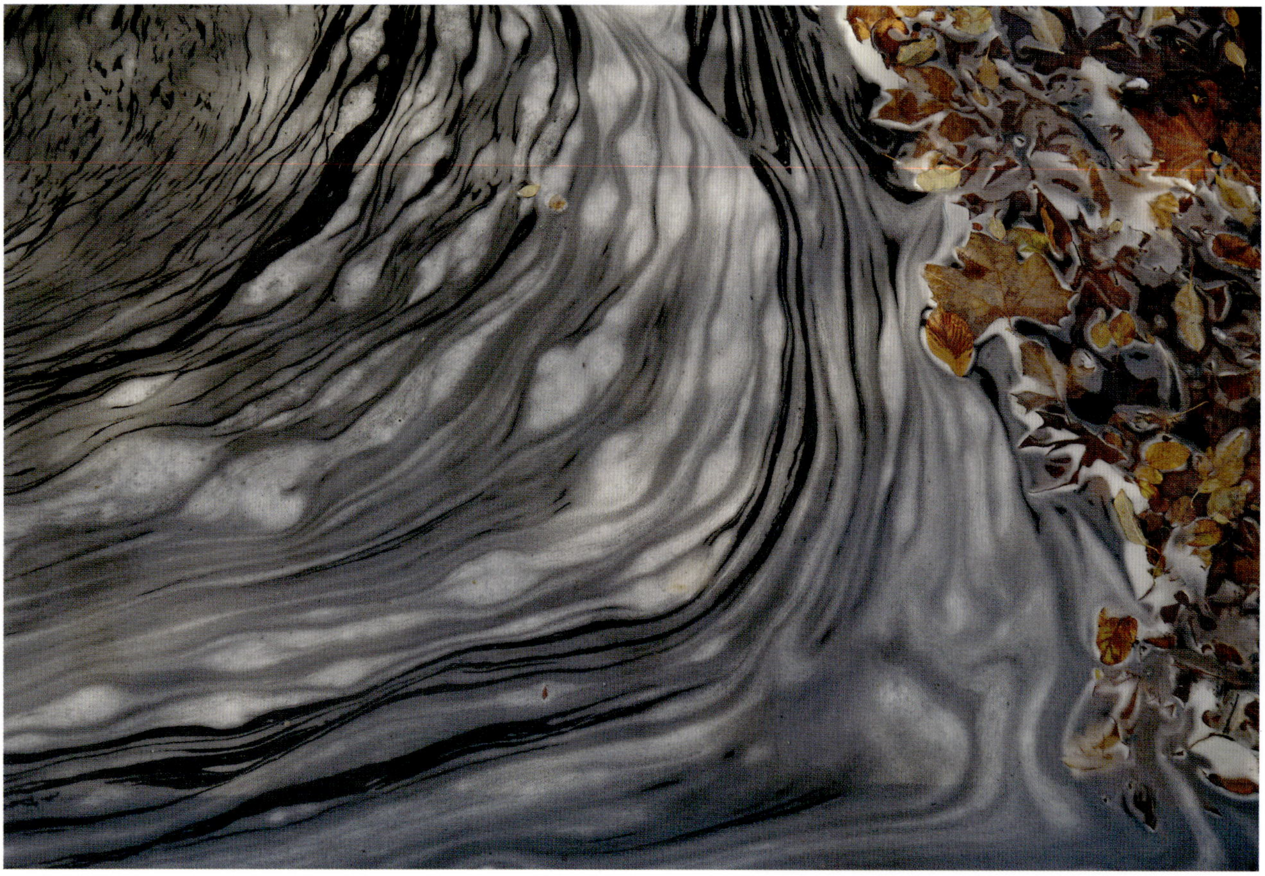

IMAGE VIEWING AS A PRACTICE   202

203 EFFORTLESS BEAUTY

IMAGE VIEWING AS A PRACTICE 204

23 When Direct Seeing Becomes Part of Who You Are

Gradually as we develop the ability to be fully present and pay attention to our world for more continuous, uninterrupted periods, we find that there is very little movement or shift in us either physically or mentally, when we see something we would like to photograph. This is because, over time, the discipline works itself into the fabric of who and how we are. We can be pulled out of any state of mind or concern, out of any discussion, by a brilliant, piercing perception. This cuts through any preoccupation that we may be having, and mercifully liberates us from the belief that our conceptual world is the only world that exists. If we are attuned to see, if our minds are fundamentally still and disciplined, if we have curiosity and passion about our world, then we become seers in the most genuine sense. The more confident we become in our ability to see, to know what we have seen, and to express this genuinely, the more quickly the process of seeing and expressing unfolds. We are stopped, we understand, we express, just like that. It can all take place very seamlessly. It can be like breathing. We breathe out as we turn our attention outwards to see, we breathe in as we receive what we have seen, and then we breathe out as we squeeze the shutter. It can be this simple. Incorporating this discipline into our lives brings about an expansion in our perspective, a softening of our territorial boundaries, and a willingness to step back from our point of view in order to take a fresh look at the subject at hand. It can mean that we know with certainty when we resonate with an image, a place, or a person, and when we do not. We are more likely to know when to walk away and when to commit further. We are grounded in our stillness: We have room to breathe, to stay steady and even as we observe and take in the entire situation, whatever it may be.

207   EFFORTLESS BEAUTY

WHEN DIRECT SEEING BECOMES PART OF WHO YOU ARE 208

EFFORTLESS BEAUTY

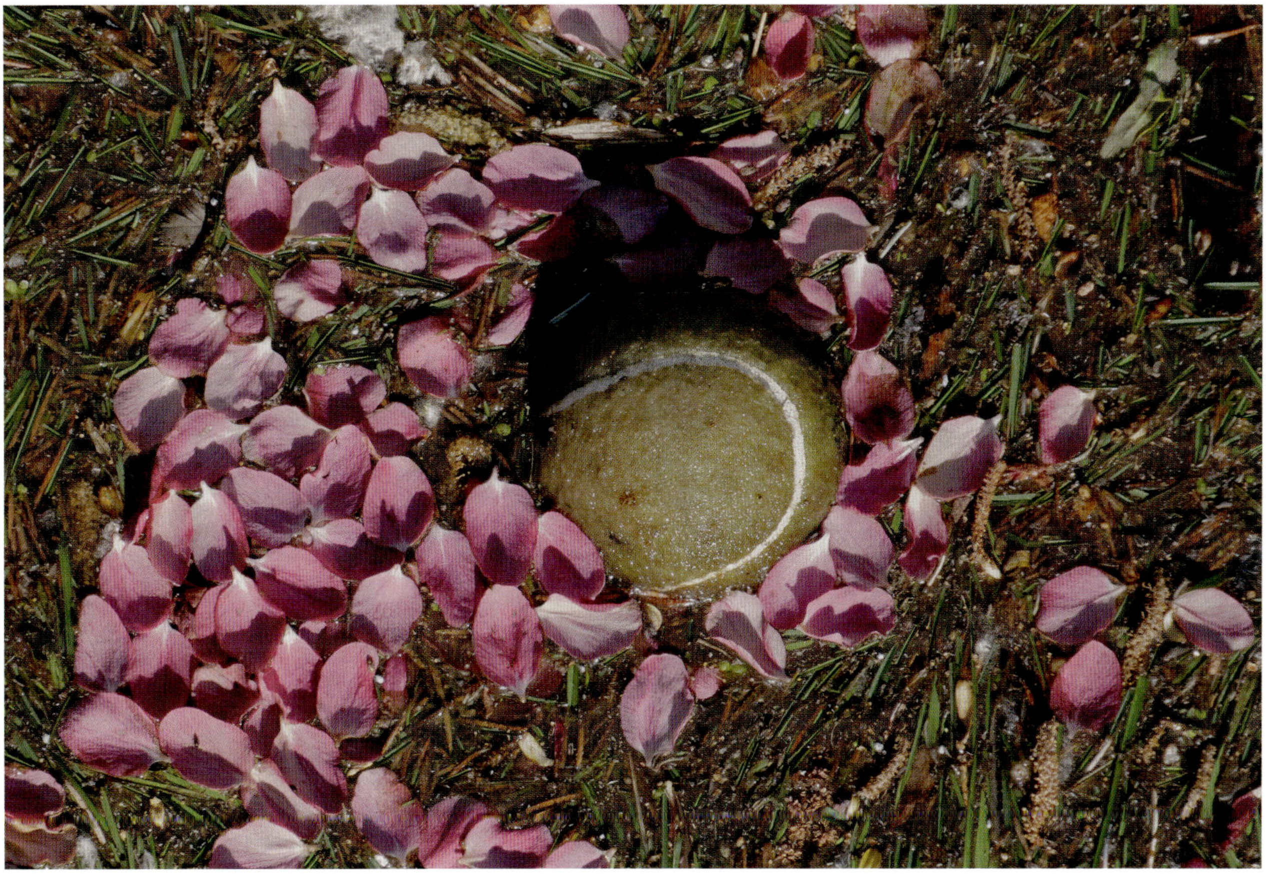

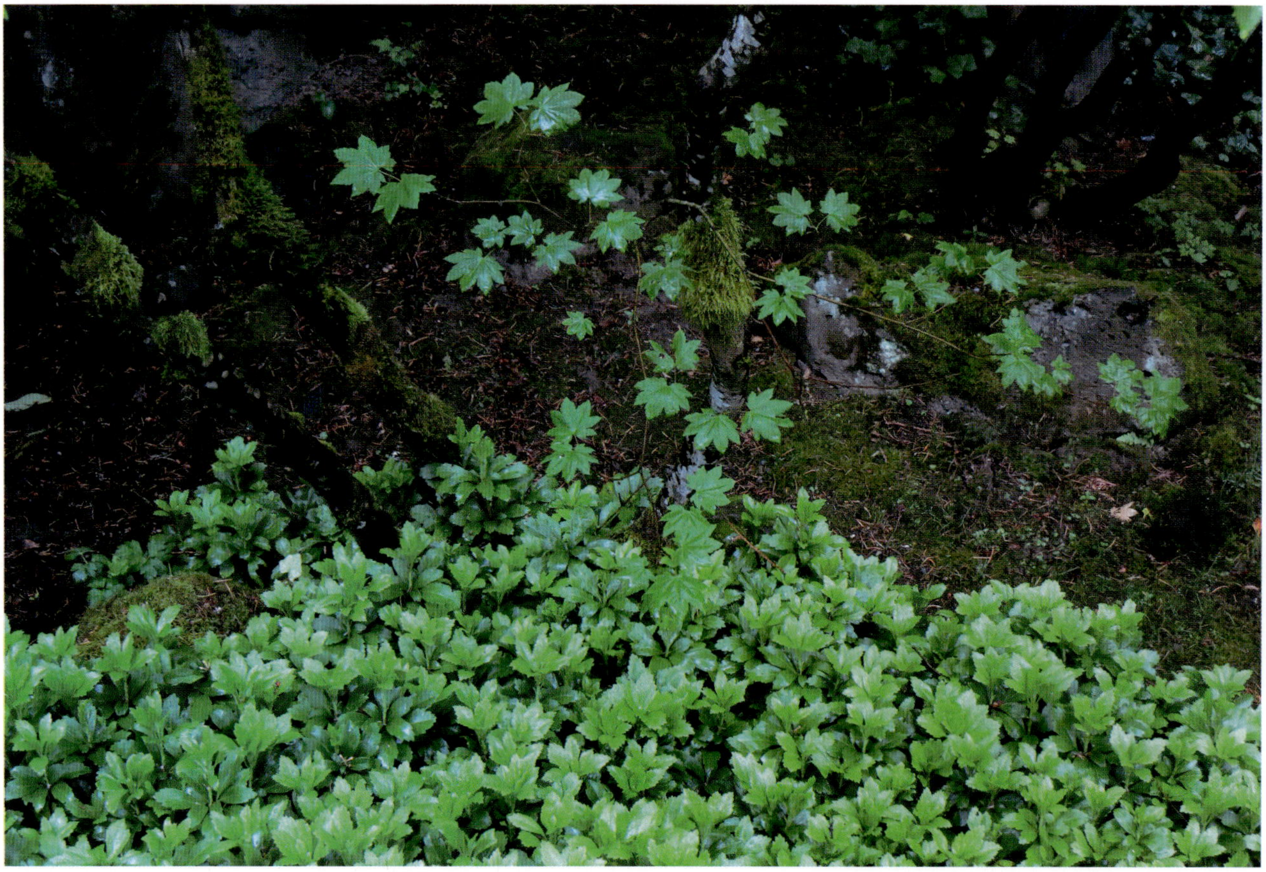

WHEN DIRECT SEEING BECOMES PART OF WHO YOU ARE   212

24   The Fully Met Life

When I contemplate how the practice of direct seeing has affected my life, the first thing that comes to my mind is the many opportunities it affords me to experience and express the totally cool things that are happening around me—the quality of the light, the breeze, the time of day, the endless coming together of color, light, and line. I can be worrying or distracted by all the details of my life that never seem to end, or I can be transported out of them suddenly, as I am penetrated by an unexpected perception, which dawns in my mind out of the blue. Noticing my world constantly disrupts my mental absorption with the linear stream of events that is my everyday life. I am reminded that beneath my preoccupations, I am vibrantly alive, and that nothing in my world is fixed and unchanging. I feel a tremendous sense of richness. I am content.

It is a sign of my passion for shooting images that I go out with my camera with the expectation that I will notice something that is surprising and often whimsical. I expect to be touched and reminded of the larger world beyond my own sense of limitation. When this happens I feel fully met, fulfilled in my relationship between my visual sense and my visual world. When a perception stops my mind I feel disoriented, ambient sounds recede, and the perceived appears brilliant, sharp and vivid. I feel joyful. What does this remind you of? Falling in love? Melting in a moment of love for your child? Feeling appreciation for your best friend in the world? Yes. In these moments I feel fully met. My partner in perception, whatever I am seeing, is not holding back, and I have no sense of shortcoming on either of our parts. I am fully engaged because I have no forethought, and no second thoughts, about how this should be, or whether or not it is good enough. In this moment, the present moment, all is complete.

I am happy and grateful that I can have a relationship like this anytime I practice direct seeing. It's like an ongoing celebration, a party where nobody has to get dressed up, and there aren't any hangovers the day after. Relationships like this make us feel wholesome and genuine. They spill over into our human relationships.

We notice more and appreciate more. We can let go of what doesn't work, any struggle we are having, and accept more easily the things that don't conform to what we think would be "better." Just as there is no such thing as half a flash, there is no question of having half a relationship. We have to be involved whole-heartedly. We are either in it or we are not.

As we connect fully with what is happening, our lives begin to change. Letting go of trying to manipulate the process of perception is the same as letting go of other things, such as our hopes and fears about what is going to happen in the next moment, that evening, the next day. We can let go of worrying about what happens when we get old, when we are sick, or whether or not our loved one will love, accept, and praise us. It's all the same thing. We are letting go of our sense that we are not good enough. As we gain confidence in our ability to take genuine photographs, we also begin to feel confident about expressing ourselves in genuine relationships.

Because we have the ability to experience our experience fully, we can act decisively, confidently. One of our students wrote us after a course and told us that her experience in the course had changed how she was relating with her husband. She said that she didn't exactly understand why, but since she began practicing direct seeing, she was more confident about expressing herself, more clear about what she wanted to express. This had greatly improved their ability to communicate with each other.

Through practicing this discipline we learn to stay open and not project our ideas and preferences onto what we are seeing. This is the essence of non-aggression, acceptance of what we experience without always judging it and determining whether it agrees with our own point of view. If we could bring this mind of equanimity to bear on situations that arise in our relationships, wouldn't the world be a more harmonious place?

I'm not saying these things and spelling them out because I want us all to feel good about working on ourselves, so that we can be better people. The practice of direct seeing is not another personal improvement project. I'm saying this because everything we do in every moment has an impact. The more we develop our ability to rest in stillness, relax our point of view, and really see and connect with our world, the more fully we will live our lives each day.

THE FULLY MET LIFE 216

EFFORTLESS BEAUTY

THE FULLY MET LIFE 218

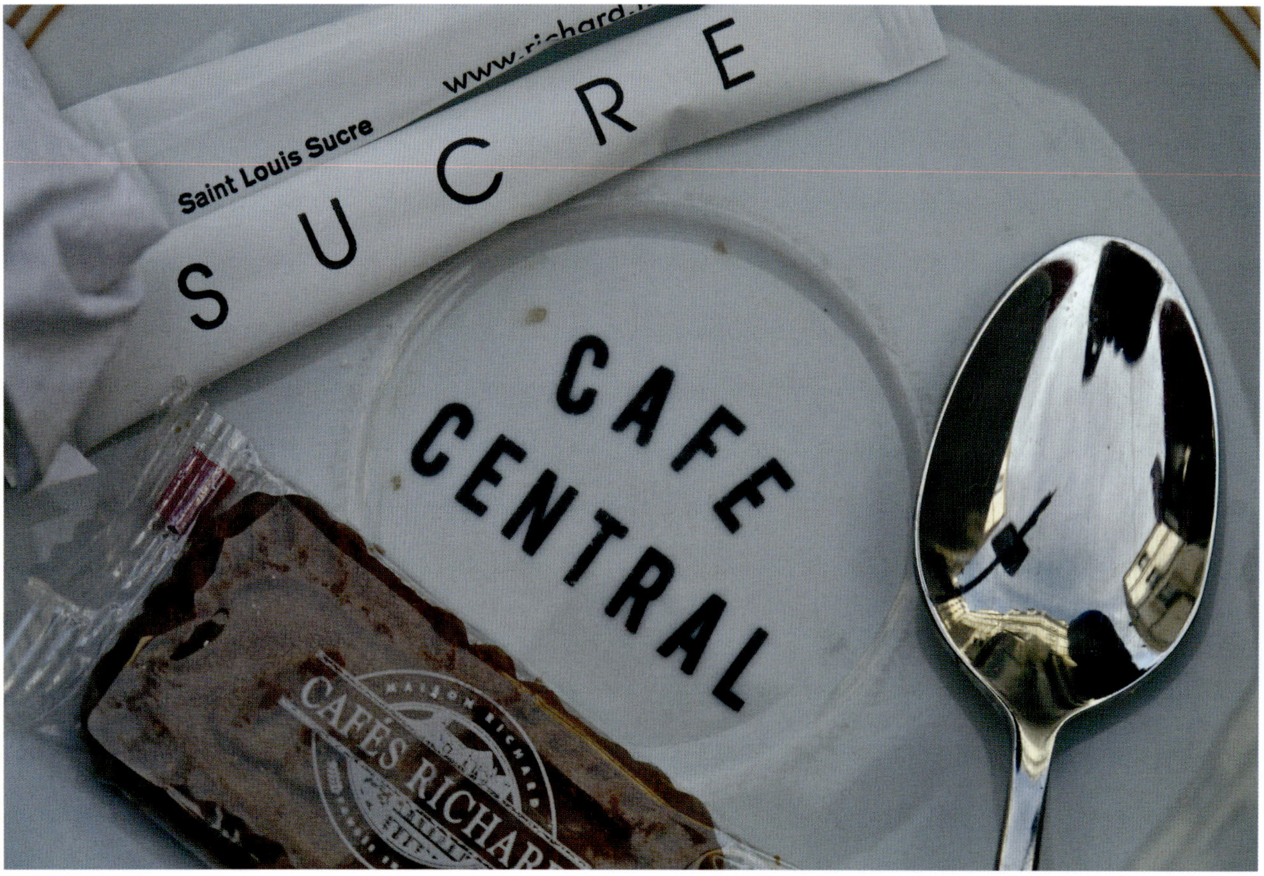
Saint Louis Sucre
SUCRE
CAFE
CENTRAL
CAFÉS RICHARD

THE FULLY MET LIFE 220

221 EFFORTLESS BEAUTY

THE FULLY MET LIFE 222

223   EFFORTLESS BEAUTY

THE FULLY MET LIFE   224

EFFORTLESS BEAUTY

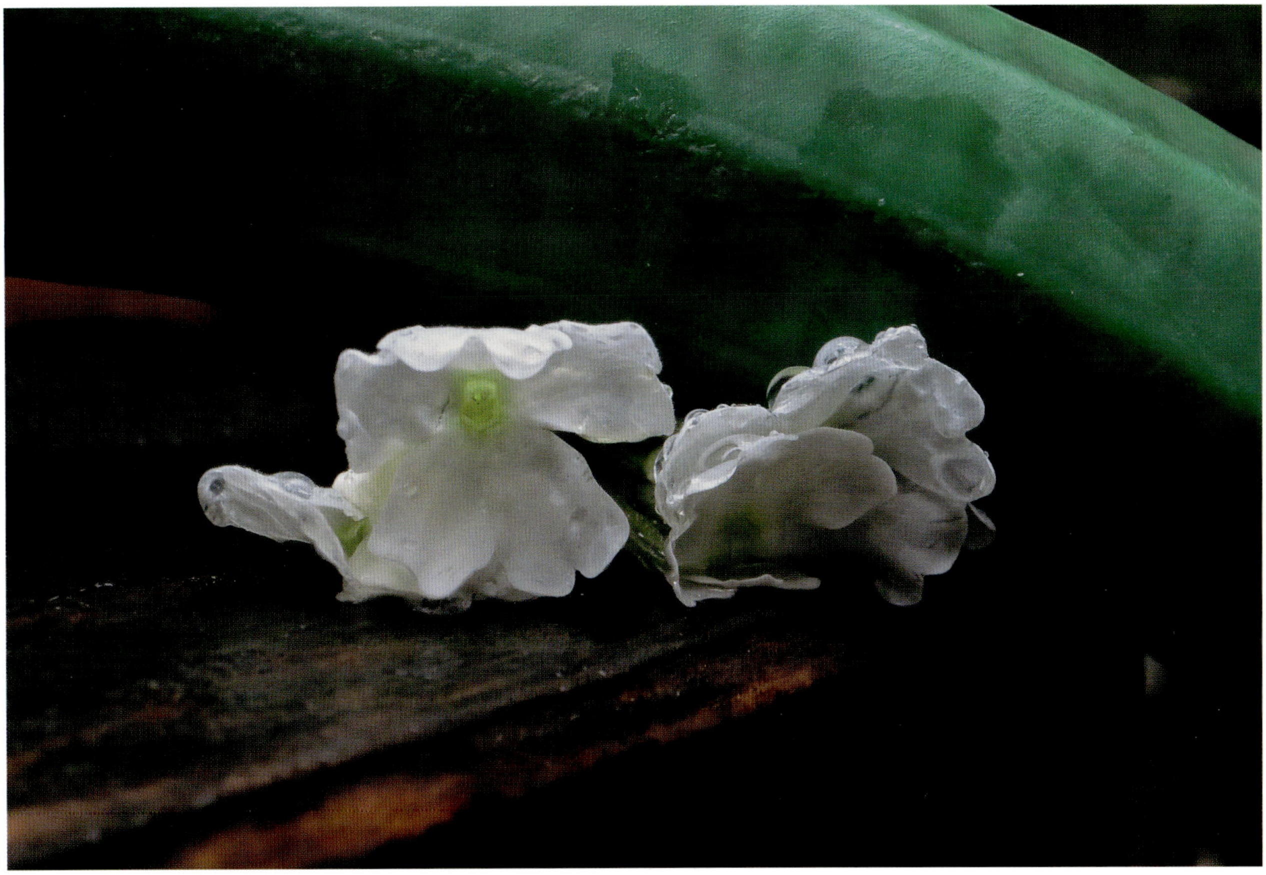

227 EFFORTLESS BEAUTY

THE FULLY MET LIFE   228

About the Author

Photograph: Paris, 2011 by Michael Wood

Julie DuBose has been a teacher of contemplative photography since 2005, and has trained with Michael Wood, the founder of the Miksang Training course of study and practice since 1998.

In 2009 she founded The Miksang Institute for Contemplative Photography in Boulder, Colorado. Julie teaches workshops throughout North America and Europe and offers an international contemplative photography intensive through the Institute each summer.

She has written numerous articles about the practice of direct perception that can be found at www.miksang.com/miksanglife.

WWW.MIKSANG.COM

Acknowledgments

I would like to express my gratitude to my Buddhist/Shambhala teacher, Chögyam Trungpa, who left a wondrous artistic legacy that continues to inspire and delight.

I would also like to thank my contemplative photography mentor and companion, Michael Wood, who continues to generate wisdom and insight about the process of fresh seeing and its expression through photography. He is an inspiration and example of discipline, gentleness, immovability, and deep resonation with genuine perception. Without him this book would simply not have been possible.

Thank you to my editor Monica Bauer, who preserved my voice and intention in my expression, and understood and appreciated the essence of my words.

May this offering bring happiness and the joy of direct perception.

Further Resources

Online Resources

www.effortlessbeautybook.com

www.miksang.com

www.miksangpublications.com

www.miksang.com/miksanglife

Recommended Reading

Andy Karr and Michael Wood, *The Practice of Contemplative Photography: Seeing the World with Fresh Eyes*, Shambhala Publications 2011.

Chögyam Trungpa, *True Perception: The Path of Dharma Art* Shambhala Publications 2008.

Permissions

Leonard Cohen quote from 'Anthem'. Used by permission.

John Lennon quote from 'Beautiful Boy (Darling Boy)'. Double Fantasy. 1980. Used by permission.

Chögyam Trungpa quotes © Diana J. Mukpo. Used by permission.

Shunryu Suzuki Roshi quotes used by permission.

Notes on the Photographs

The photos in this book were taken in the following places:

Amsterdam, The Netherlands
Aspen, Colorado
Boise, Idaho
Boulder, Colorado
Cologne, Germany
Crestone, Colorado
Delray Beach, Florida
Denver, Colorado
Halifax, Nova Scotia
Los Angeles, California
Lyons, Colorado
Palm Beach, Florida
Paris, France
Portland Oregon
Toronto, Canada
Tucson, Arizona
Vancouver, British Columbia
Victoria, British Columbia
Zandvoort Beach, The Netherlands

Equipment used for these photographs:

Canon T3i
Canon 50mm f.1.4 lens
Canon 24-105mm f.4.0 L-Series lens
Canon 70-200mm f.4.0 L-Series lens

Panasonic Lumix G3
Leica 50mm f.1.4 lens
Leica 90mm Macro f.2.0 lens
Lumix G-Vario 90 – 300mm lens

Canon S-100
Panasonic Lumix FZ-100